Praise for *Get Out of My Head*

"As a world-class distance swimmer turned successful entrepreneur, Andrew McConnell knows what it takes to keep your cool under pressure. As an author, he knows how to get you fired up about Stoic wisdom. Thanks to his engaging stories and practical advice, you won't have any trouble getting out of your head and into this book."

—Adam Grant, #1 *New York Times* bestselling author of *Think Again* and host of the TED podcast *WorkLife*

"*Get Out of My Head* offers an authentic solution for those struggling to cut through the din of overly busy modern lives and accomplish more."

—Dr. Bernice A. King, CEO of the Martin Luther King Jr. Center for Nonviolent Social Change

"*Get Out of My Head* will help you overcome stress and let you feel in control of your mind. If you follow the ideas in this book, your life will become substantially better. A fantastic read that will make you more focused and productive—I highly recommend it."

—Chris Bailey, international bestselling author of *Hyperfocus* and *The Productivity Project*

GET

OUT

OF MY

HEAD

GET OUT OF MY HEAD

Creating Modern Clarity with Stoic Wisdom

M. Andrew McConnell

Matt Holt Books
An Imprint of BenBella Books, Inc.
Dallas, TX

Matt Holt Books is an imprint of BenBella Books, Inc.
10440 N. Central Expressway
Suite 800
Dallas, TX 75231
benbellabooks.com
Send feedback to feedback@benbellabooks.com.

BenBella and *Matt Holt* are federally registered trademarks.

Printed in the United States of America
10 9 8 7 6 5 4 3 2 1

Library of Congress Control Number: 2021057344
ISBN 9781637740750 (trade cloth)
ISBN 9781637740767 (electronic)

Editing by Rachel Phares
Copyediting by Jennifer Brett Greenstein
Proofreading by Lisa Story and Cape Cod Compositors, Inc.
Indexing by WordCo Indexing Services, Inc.
Text design and composition by PerfecType, Nashville, TN
Cover design by Brigid Pearson
Printed by Lake Book Manufacturing

To the Llama and my Sweet Pea. You inspire me every day to work to become the person you already believe me to be.

CONTENTS

PROLOGUE

On a brisk October day in 2009, David Cummings, an Atlanta software entrepreneur, made the fabled pilgrimage to the heart of Silicon Valley. In the tech world, Sand Hill Road is the Mount Olympus of venture investing, and the man David and his cofounder, Adam Blitzer, were there to meet was Zeus.

David and Adam arrived at Bill Gurley's office at the venture capital firm Benchmark with the hope of securing funding for their software company. Bill was an imposing figure, both as a titan in the VC world and by virtue of his sheer size: a former basketball player at the University of Florida, he stood six feet and nine inches tall. Bill stepped into the conference room and introduced himself to his guests, towering over the slender software entrepreneurs, their concave shoulders a product of countless hours spent in front of their computer screens. Once the awkward pleasantries were out of the way, the three men sat down around a mahogany table, as sturdy and imposing as Bill Gurley's handshake.

David had woken up that morning feeling good about the pitch; he knew he had a compelling story to tell. He was a serial entrepreneur with a number of revenue-generating companies under his belt. His latest venture, and the reason he and his business partner had come to Silicon Valley, was a software company called Pardot that was bringing in more than $1 million a year in revenue, having quadrupled in size over the past year alone. Even better, Pardot had managed this without raising a single dollar of outside money. But for all of his confidence upon entering the meeting, now that he was there, in the large conference room across from an imposing venture capitalist, David could not shake the nervousness that came with feeling like he did not belong. This was David's state of mind as he dove into his presentation, hoping the trembling of his hands and voice was not apparent to Bill Gurley.

When the pitch was finally over, David waited expectantly for Bill's response, praying for the validation—and the investment—he had come all this way for. The venture capitalist remained silent, taking a sip from an espresso cup that looked like a child's teacup in his enormous hands. David's heart was racing and the sound of blood rushing in his ears was so loud that when Bill finally spoke, David had to read his lips to understand what he was saying.

"Are y'all sure you want to raise money?" After a beat, Bill's thick Texan drawl came through to David's senses.

The answer to Bill's question seemed so obvious. Of course, David wanted funding. He was here, wasn't he? David sat silently. His confusion must have registered, because Bill Gurley proceeded to break down the question with actual numbers. Unfolding a napkin on the table and grabbing a pen, Bill held court.

He went on, "Pardot grew by four times last year and thinks it will grow another three times next year, and another three times the year after that. Now, Pardot can't keep that up forever . . . so let's assume it slows down to doubling the year after that, and then growing 50 percent the year after that. At Pardot's current margin, and the multiples such a business is likely to attract, Pardot should be able to sell for $50 million. And if you do that without raising any outside money, you won't have to share the proceeds with anyone."

The entrepreneurs nodded, not wanting to interrupt this master class in venture math. Bill continued, "On the other hand, let's assume Pardot goes down the path of raising venture capital. Once Pardot is on that treadmill, it is almost impossible to get off. In each round of financing, Pardot will have to sell 20 to 30 percent of its business. Every round is geared toward getting Pardot to the next round faster, thus accelerating how soon it will again have to sell an additional chunk of itself. Yes, the eventual exit value of the company might be bigger, but the founders' take is likely to be much lower. And you are going to start losing control of the company you founded the day you take that first outside money. Is that really what you want?"

Bill's question stupefied the entrepreneurs.

This was not what David or his cofounder wanted at all: that much was now obvious, written in black ink on the white paper napkin in front of them. In a daze, the entrepreneurs thanked Bill for his time, surrendered their hands once more to be engulfed by his, and walked out of the office, leaving Bill Gurley, Benchmark, and Sand Hill Road in all their majesty behind them.

The following week, back in Atlanta, David thought about the advice Bill Gurley had proffered. In an Excel spreadsheet, he modeled different scenarios of Pardot's trajectory over the course of an afternoon; indeed, what took David hours of painstaking modeling to conclude, Bill had surmised in less than five minutes on that damn napkin!

After that meeting, David realized that his mind, as well as his desires for himself and his company, had been hijacked by the tech press. He had seen the media celebrate companies that reported multimillion-dollar investments and ignore those that grew self-sufficiently, and had unconsciously allowed outside forces to set his goals for him and his company. Drinking the Kool-Aid, David had wrongly identified investment figures as the measure of success. Although he'd built his company based on entrepreneurial excitement and his belief in the value it could bring to customers, along the way he'd gotten lost in the need for a specific form of external validation—investment from a big West Coast venture capital firm. David's meeting at Benchmark had recalibrated his professional priorities by helping him create mental boundaries and eliminate the outside noise.

• • • • • •

Almost two years to the day of his meeting with Bill Gurley, David woke up to learn that one of Pardot's biggest competitors had just raised a whopping $50 million in venture capital. By tech industry standards, this was a huge success—and a crushing blow to Pardot. How could it possibly compete? What could its future be now that it had to contend with the comically deep pockets of its rival company?

But this was not two years ago.

David knew he had to address the threat with his team. And so, walking into the office, he called an all-hands-on-deck meeting. Remembering the lesson about internal versus external measures of success he'd taken to heart after his meeting at Benchmark, he explained that there were two ways he and his team could respond. They could give their minds to their competitor, making decisions only in reaction to what their rival was doing, or *might* do, or they could double down on themselves—on the competitive advantages their position now gave them.

He could see the skeptical glances of Pardot's employees darting around the room, as well as a few pockets of employees furtively whispering in the back. Undoubtedly, they were thinking that $50 million was a pretty big competitive advantage. David went on.

Deep pockets can make a company inefficient. Pardot had already gleaned evidence of this, having competed head-to-head with this rival that, after all, had been venture-backed nearly the entire time. With venture investment dollars in its bank account, this competitor had been able to offer discounts that led to financial losses; add new features to its software that customers did not need, want, or understand; and throw bodies at problems, like client onboarding, rather than solve issues through automation and product innovation. Yes, Pardot's now-even-more-well-funded adversary was going to be able to do even more with its new money, things that Pardot—funded by its customers, not West Coast venture capitalists—was simply unable to match. But rather than looking at this as a disadvantage, David explained how it played right into Pardot's hands.

Pardot had a competitive price and a "Southern nice" approach, in David's words, whereby it always focused on being helpful, not pushy. This meant that Pardot had industry-leading customer retention, whereas its larger competitor had a reputation as "used car salespeople" and was known to be aggressive with discounts and pressure tactics. The Pardot team members had to lean into their own strengths; they could not allow themselves to get distracted by their competitor's financial backing. They needed to stay focused on delivering features that clients not only needed but also valued and were willing to pay for. They could not allow themselves to get caught up in a rat race for venture capital investment.

No, David would not allow this rival company to build a home in Pardot's proverbial headspace. He would not throw Pardot onto the perpetual hamster wheel that was the pursuit of venture capital dollars. He instead implored his team members to act on the lesson he had learned from Bill Gurley two years prior—the power of setting mental boundaries, of dictating what they allowed to permeate their minds and how they chose to define success. This meant they would continue to do what they did best—providing their customers with an excellent, easy-to-use product and extraordinary service—without getting caught up in how their competitors were doing business.

Ultimately, under David's leadership, Pardot responded to the news of its rival's funding by making its product even simpler and easier to use and by investing in a seamless, automated onboarding process that provided value to its clients and kept Pardot's costs for customer acquisition far below that of its competitors. The result? In head-to-head sales, where Pardot and the other company went after the same client, Pardot won far more than it lost, shallower pockets notwithstanding.

David's story illustrates how common it is for us—even our brightest and most accomplished—to let people, events, circumstances, and even nonexistent versions of ourselves live rent-free in our minds, and to unconsciously use that external input as the default when it comes to making decisions for ourselves. It also demonstrates the power of doing the opposite: putting a real, meaningful value on our minds and proactively policing their borders, allowing us to set our own priorities based on what's actually best for us.

· · · · · ·

What David didn't know at the time, but would come to understand, is that the practice of valuing and zealously guarding the mind has ancient roots. These concepts were first introduced around 300 BC with the genesis of Stoicism—an ancient school of philosophy that advocated a kind of mental discipline and detachment from external forces. Those who abided by these principles were known as Stoics. They included Zeno of Citium (Stoicism's founder), Epictetus, Seneca, Marcus Aurelius, and many more. Two millennia later, through several twists and turns and a headful of doubt, David had learned how to navigate his career like a Stoic. Leveraging this mindset, he would go on to take Pardot, as well as a number of other companies, to even greater heights, but more on that later.

David is proof that no matter how accustomed you are to giving away your headspace, it's still possible to take back ownership of your mind in order to achieve clarity, make good decisions, and rise in your career. Yet David is just one of many modern Stoics, applying ancient mental practices in today's world of work. All of us have what is necessary to become a Stoic of our own work and lives. What it takes is an owner's mindset and some good old ancient discipline.

INTRODUCTION

Like most first-time entrepreneurs, I had a vision of what starting my first company would be like: No one would be telling me what to do anymore—I'd be my own boss. It was going to mean complete freedom, including control over my time and workload, and I couldn't wait.

Like most first-time entrepreneurs, I was dead wrong.

Sure, I no longer worked for someone else. Now I was working for what seemed like *everyone* else. When it feels like every single client can make or break your entire endeavor, the stress of keeping them happy far exceeds what some annoying boss in a corporate job may elicit.

As my company grew (which is exactly what I wanted, right?), that freedom I thought I'd be gaining by working for myself seemed to become only more elusive. The larger my company got, the more people I had to be accountable to; rather than just being the errand boy of my clients, I now had to answer to my employees, my investors, our industry partners, and more. Instead of having one boss who "took away my freedom," I had seemingly countless bosses doing so, and the number was only growing.

To make matters worse, not only was the freedom I thought I would get in my working day by founding and running my own company a mirage, but I was also losing my nights and weekends to work. And it wasn't just the crazy hours I worked. Even during the times when I was "off the clock," I couldn't stop thinking about the client who was unhappy, the employees who were not getting along with one another, the investor who was losing patience, or the prospective partner we were negotiating an agreement with who was asking for unrealistic terms. When I worked for someone else, work could more easily stay at work. Now that I supposedly worked for myself, I, or at least my mind, seemed to stay at work 24/7. Ironically, my time, my schedule, and my mind seemed to be out of my own control.

Thankfully, that is not how I live my life now. Instead of living frantically beholden to the needs and desires of others at the expense of my own freedom and sanity, I set my own boundaries and priorities, and I'm much happier—and more successful—for it. What changed? I will let you in on a secret. It wasn't my clients or my company's partners. It wasn't my employees. It wasn't even my investors. It was *me*.

My "aha" moment came because I was so entrenched in my work that I couldn't think of anything else. My company, Rented, helps property owners and managers make the most of their vacation homes and investment properties in the short-term rental market. Just as our company had figured out how to successfully maximize the value of our clients' most expensive or second-most-expensive assets, I finally realized that I could be making far more of *my* most valuable asset, and it was one I had completely neglected in my own life: my mind.

Just as we helped our clients see that they had historically undersold the true value of their real estate assets, I came to realize I was not just underselling my mind, but actually giving it away entirely for free to anyone who asked—and to many who did not. What's more, by giving my mind away for free, I was effectively relegating myself to the status of a renter in my own mind. Here was the one asset in life that I should own, the only asset I ever really *could* own, and yet I spent my time accessing only the remnants of what was left after others had taken what I'd given away all too freely.

Perhaps even more tragically, my mind wasn't an asset I'd had to spend a lifetime building up wealth to acquire. Unlike physical real estate, which we must work for years to be able to afford and own if we're not born trust fund babies, mental real estate doesn't require financial wealth or hefty loans to acquire it. We're all born with the same incredible inheritance of riches when it comes to our mental real estate. We own it free and clear from the day we are born. And yet, we seem to default to squandering this inheritance. Indeed, as we grow older and supposedly wiser, we often give away our mental resources more readily, forcing ourselves into the position of becoming renters of our own minds.

But just because we have become renters—rather than owners—of our minds does not mean we have to stay that way. We all have the ability to take back our time and energy and reassert ownership of our *truly* most valuable asset. And while doing this requires at least as much work and dedication as it takes to acquire and accumulate physical real estate, the outcome is ultimately in our control, and the payoff is well worth it.

Ancient Wisdom

As with so many of my "original" thoughts and insights, I soon discovered I wasn't the first person to come to the realization that my mind was like valuable real estate that I was giving away too cheaply. In the words of Alfred North Whitehead, "Everyone is the unconscious proponent of some philosopher."[1] In this particular instance, the originators of the concept beat me not by a few years but rather by a few *thousand*. They were the ancient Stoics, and their way of looking at the world, at life, and at human potential could not be more relevant for us today.

As Seneca stated so well in the first century of the common era, in his essay "On the Shortness of Life":

> Were all the geniuses of history to focus on this single theme, they could never fully express their bafflement at the darkness of the human mind. *No person would give up even an inch of their estate, and the slightest dispute with a neighbor can mean hell to pay; yet we easily let others encroach on our lives—worse, we often pave the way for those who will take it over.* No person hands out their money to passersby, but to how many do each of us hand out our lives! *We're tight-fisted with property and money, yet think too little of wasting time, the one thing about which we should all be the toughest misers.* [italics added]

Though these words were written thousands of years ago, they likely still apply to most of us. Think about it. Have you ever let someone get under your skin, thinking back to a snide comment or act on their part for hours, if not days, afterward?

Have you found yourself at home, supposedly having dinner with your family, while your mind remained completely at the office as you replayed some event from earlier in the day?

Have you ever found yourself lying in bed and unable to sleep on a Sunday night because you can't stop the movie in your mind of all the things that you're going to be responsible for in the coming week?

These are just a handful of the limitless examples that illustrate the common state Seneca lamented because when we hand over our minds, we are indeed handing over our lives. When we give others control over our minds and, in turn, our minds have control over us, we're incapable of living our lives on our own terms. We're robbed of experiencing and enjoying life as we want to, and instead we live in reaction to others. All of these behaviors are completely normal—they are also unhelpful and completely unnecessary.

Why, you might ask, *in the twenty-first century, should I bother turning to what a few old men said thousands of years ago?*

Sure, the time the ancient Stoics lived in was different from our own. There was no electricity. There were no planes, trains, or automobiles. There weren't mobile phones or computers, and no one talked about the threat of artificial intelligence or machine learning taking over humans' very purpose for existence. And yet, the human condition, especially the mental condition, remains the same. These philosophers' insights on what holds us back as humans, and how to break those mental chains, are just as relevant now as they were then—and perhaps more so, as I hope you will see. These old men are not our masters, but they can certainly be masterful guides.

In our own time, as people humblebrag about their busyness with worrying regularity, Seneca is there to remind us that this is not just a problem of the modern world: During his own time, he noted that a common complaint was "I have no chance to live." His response? As he writes in "On the Shortness of Life," "Of course you have no chance! All those who summon you to themselves, turn you away from your own self . . . Check off, I say, and review the days of your life; you will see that very few, and those the refuse, have been left for you." In other words, when you spend all your mental energy in ways that others want you to spend that energy, you steal precious time from yourself.

Still not convinced?

Then hear it from someone closer to our own time. Sam Altman, CEO of OpenAI and the former president of Y Combinator, the startup factory that was an early backer of companies like Airbnb, DoorDash, Instacart, Dropbox, and more, advised his followers on Twitter, "Don't let jerks live rent-free in your head."[2]

Not there yet? Then take this from the most prescient pop philosopher of our time, Taylor Swift, who laments in her song "I Forgot That You Existed" that, rather than moving on, she spent too many days thinking about how a former lover did her wrong, wrong, wrong, with "free rent, living in my mind."[3]

The point is, you're not alone if you feel like you are a mere tenant of your mind, having to rent the remnants of what is left after everyone else has taken their share of it. Everyone from ancient philosophers to some of the most well-known and successful people of our own time has dealt with this problem. The good news is, it's as common as it is avoidable, preventable, and addressable.

As the often-richest person in the world pointed out in his 2003 shareholder letter, "Owners are different from tenants." Jeff Bezos was and still is right. Now it is time we all heed his admonition: "Here's to not being a tenant!"

Our Caveman Mind

I imagine you might now be wondering why, if it seems that everyone agrees that letting others control our time and headspace leads to feeling miserable and overworked, this state of mental tenancy remains nearly universal. The answer lies in human evolution. As James Clear, the number-one *New York Times* best-selling author of *Atomic Habits*, points out in his essay "The Evolution of Anxiety: Why We Worry and What to Do About It," for the vast majority of human existence our ancestors lived in an "immediate-return environment"[4]—meaning that for roughly 197,500 years of our 200,000-year existence as a species, we lived and evolved in a world where most of the choices we made had an immediate impact on our lives. Our ancestors were quite literally focused on their day-to-day survival—securing food and shelter and avoiding predators. As a necessity of existence, they were focused on the present moment.

It was only relatively recently, beginning around 2,500 years ago, that our human ancestors found themselves instead living in a "delayed return environment." As Clear explains:

> Most of the choices you make today will not benefit you immediately. If you do a good job at work today, you'll get a paycheck in a few weeks. If you save money now, you'll have enough for retirement later. Many aspects of modern society are designed to delay rewards until some point in the future . . . many of the problems humans worry about are problems of the future.

In other words, we've gotten used to spending our mental energy thinking and worrying about things that have yet to happen. Why is this such a problem? Simply put, because our brains have not evolved to solve the problems we face in this kind of environment.

Let's put some numbers behind this. The average person can read five words per second. In data terms, this means our conscious minds are able to process an average of fifty bits of data per second. To put this into perspective, human senses have evolved to take in *eleven million bits of data per second* from our environment. So every second we spend reading, that eleven million bits our senses take in are processed and condensed down to the fifty bits our conscious minds can absorb. Our brains have evolved to be able to process a relatively small amount of data to keep us alive—the ultimate measure of a species' success in an immediate-return environment. In the savanna, it didn't necessarily matter that the blue sky was starting to get cloudy, that the wind was picking up and getting colder, or that it was starting to get darker earlier in the day. All that mattered was that the rustling over there might be a lion. Our ancestors had to be able to filter those eleven million bits down to the truly critical fifty bits they needed to stay alive *right now*. They didn't have time to think through the best time of year to plant crops in order to have sufficient food in several months; they had to survive the next few minutes, or even seconds.

But now we are out of the savanna. Now we are in metropolises with totally different demands on us, and on our minds. And to put it mildly, our brains are ill-equipped for the world in which we find ourselves.

That's the bad news—and unfortunately the problem is only getting worse. Historically, we had to contend with just the data filtering through our senses in our natural environment. Now, data are being created at a pace and on a scale never before experienced. I mean this literally: More data were created in the years 2015 and 2016 than in the previous five thousand years of human history combined. In 2017, more data were created than in the previous two years combined. And the speed of data creation has only accelerated since then. It's no wonder our minds are stretched so thin.

To go back to the real estate analogy, I was recently speaking with a friend, a successful investor in both physical real estate and the technology companies that are transforming the real estate industry more broadly. On the subject of COVID-19 and its damaging economic aftershocks, he lamented that between the 2008 financial crisis and what many suffered due to the pandemic in 2020 and beyond, we were going to see an entire generation of "perpetual renters" who will never have the financial means or stability to own their own homes.

The overwhelming creation of data we've seen in recent years is creating the same situation with our mental real estate. One example of this is "doomscrolling"—the tendency to mindlessly scroll through bad news online—which has dominated how many people spend their "free time." This is just one of many ways in which we've been complicit in creating a world of perpetual mind renters, who are unable to seize ownership of this most valuable and critical asset.

If that's the bad news, the good news is that just because being a mind renter is normal, is understandable, and is even scientifically explainable doesn't mean that it has to remain our default state. Just as (in a perfect world) an apartment renter can become a homeowner by building financial wealth, so too can a mind renter become an owner of their own mind by building mental affluence.

The even better news is that, unlike financial affluence, mental affluence is completely within our control. We're not dependent on a privileged upbringing, or a boss to hire us or give us a raise, or even a customer to buy a new product we invented, to build our mental affluence. We all have the power and the ability to retake ownership of what's rightfully ours. It really is that simple—however, achieving this is far from easy.

Making It Real

In this book I share the stories of some of the most successful and inspiring people I know who have gotten to where they are by successfully taking ownership of their minds. These people are modern Stoics: people who, despite all the biology fighting against them, have managed to avoid falling prey to mental tenancy and thus have been able to take ownership of their minds to great effect. They have gone on to succeed in corporate and startup environments, in the private and the public sectors, in the arts and in war (literally), in athletic and sedentary endeavors, and more.

Their stories demonstrate the possibility and power of mind ownership. They illustrate how, if you want to own your life, it's not enough to just own the time on your calendar; you must be able to decide and control *where* you mentally are during any given block of time. These success stories don't suggest you keep the entire world out, living in selfish isolation in order to take back ownership of your mind. Instead, they show that you can (and should) still invite guests into your mental real estate, and you can even rent your mind to others—it's just that doing so must be an active decision, not a passive default state. In fact, by giving up this mental real estate mindfully you can make more of your mind and your life—including your career and your relationships—than you perhaps ever thought possible.

When it comes to life as a mind renter, there are three main groups we find ourselves passively renting *from* rather than consciously deciding when and how to rent *to*: other people, events and circumstances beyond our control, and different versions of ourselves. This is why *Get Out of My Head* is structured as it is. **Part I, "Mind Renting and Other People,"** is about how to stop renting from others what you already own. **Part II, "Mind Renting and Circumstances and Events,"** takes this a step further, recognizing that it isn't always people who are the problem. Sometimes, even oftentimes, it's "life" and its unpredictability and uncontrollability that get in the way. **Part III, "Mind Renting and Ourselves,"** wraps up by tackling the most pernicious, and the most difficult to overcome, of the three groups from which we're renting headspace: different versions of ourselves. These other versions of us could be imagined versions, past or future versions, or versions we think we should be; the flavors are almost limitless. However, the commonality is that none of these versions are the "us" of now, the only us that actually exists and can ever exist.

Each chapter will introduce the most common mental tenancy problems faced with these groups, and then provide actionable solutions to overcome them. I'll also share my own corresponding "aha" moment—how I got something so wrong, and the negative impact it had on my life, personally and professionally—to make it easier for you to identify the commonalities with your own current situation. Each chapter then explains the Stoic principle of mind ownership that breaks the negative cycle and habit, discusses the scientific reasons why this principle is true and helpful, and features the principle at work in historical and contemporary examples of some of the most successful and impressive people ever to live.

The hope is that all of this will elicit your own "aha" moment, one in which you achieve your own flash of clarity in identifying both a problem and what the potential solution can look like. But we won't stop there—the purpose of this book isn't to just share the information (G.I. Joe was correct when he said that knowing is only half the battle). As Shannon Lee writes in *Be Water, My Friend: The True Teachings of Bruce Lee*:

> Sometimes it's easy to have a revelation and forget to incorporate it into your life. Aha moments are awesome! They feel really good, and while you may think about them often, that doesn't mean you follow through on them and live them proactively.[5]

This is why every single chapter closes by providing a tactical tool, worksheet, or framework that you can start applying *right now* in your quest to transition from mind renter to mind owner. If knowing is half the battle, the other half comes from action. The tools that close each chapter provide the action plan you'll need, but only you can begin to implement it in your own life.

Let the Games Begin

Up to this point, you may have unintentionally resigned yourself to life as a mind renter. It's a very natural state, and in fact the default state for our brains at this period in human history. Now, however, you know that the "default" is not the only answer. It's also not the right answer. By picking up this book, you have already demonstrated that it's no longer the answer for you.

As James Baldwin said, albeit in a different context, until this point you have been "playing the game according to somebody else's rules, and you can't win until you understand the rules and step out of that particular game, which is not, after all, worth playing."[6] It's time to step out of this game designed by someone else and start making your own. In the game that's your life, it's time you play to win.

PART I
. . . .

Mind Renting and Other People

CHAPTER 1

· ·

They'll Never Buy the Cow If You Give Them the Milk for Free (*Know Your Value*)

You can't expect others to value you if
you don't know how to value yourself.

I t was Memorial Day weekend, and I sat hunched over my computer screen. The timing was, theoretically, perfect for me to get some work done. My wife was at the pool with our daughter and our friends enjoying the sunny weather, some hot dogs, the company, and likely a cold beverage or two. That meant I had all this time to myself to work.

In front of me were multiple Excel sheets and too many open browser tabs to count, each containing the data I sought. Slowly, manually, laboriously, I copied that data piece by piece into the relevant Excel sheets. As my eyes watered from staring unblinkingly at my computer screen, I kept myself going with the knowledge that this would be the basis for what would become my company's annual "Rented Report of the Best Places to Invest in Vacation Homes." Ever since reading about how Barbara

Corcoran credited her "Corcoran Report" for helping her business take off, I thought a similar report for our sector could help do the same for my business. That had been months ago, but there was no movement toward the creation of such a report in my company. Until now, that is.

I'd shared the idea with my marketing team as soon as I read Barbara's story. They'd nodded and smiled. Every week or two I would notice we still did not have the report, and I would bring it up again. They all agreed it would be a great idea, but again, no movement. Tired of the stagnation, I'd decided to grind through it myself on a holiday weekend. That's what an entrepreneur does, right?

As I write this, our "Rented Report" is in its sixth year. Each year it gets picked up by numerous media outlets like *Forbes* and *USA Today*, and it remains the single largest generator of new leads for our business. This is a success story, of course. Clearly, spending that holiday weekend away from my friends and family was the right thing to do. Or was it?

Seneca famously wrote that "each man regards nothing as cheaper than himself." That Memorial Day weekend in 2016, I was valuing myself, and my time, at less than zero. It was a disservice to my company, my family, and myself. Why?

To start, did that project really need to be completed over a holiday weekend? I'd had the idea for it months prior. Surely there had been time earlier, and surely there would be time later, to do the necessary work. Thinking about the value of my time, I wondered if there was any time more costly than what I'd forfeited in not enjoying a holiday with my family and friends. That was time I was never getting back. Was it worth giving up for this one task?

Next, did it have to be me pulling the data? I had a marketing team, didn't I? Why hadn't they done it? Well, because I never really asked. As annoyed as I was, running an inner monologue in my head all weekend about how they made me spend my weekend doing this monotonous work, I had to eventually come to terms with the fact that I had never explicitly asked them to do it in the first place. They each had full-time jobs. They had work they were responsible for. They had no way of knowing that this particular harebrained idea I had was something I wanted and expected them to follow through on.

And lastly, the perfect illustration of just how I viewed "nothing as cheaper than myself" in that particular instance is that in future years I deemed the work of compiling the report to be below the pay grade of my own team. Once I took a step back and realized how repetitive the data gathering was and that it did not require any real judgment, I simply hired contractors through Upwork to do the work for me at an incredibly cheap hourly rate. Then, after a couple of years doing that, I worked with our development team to automate the process entirely. I eventually literally determined that this work was not valuable enough for another human to do, other than me, of course. My own time, my own holiday weekend, I treated as the cheapest resource available, although it is the most finite resource I possess.

This behavior is not unique to me. But perhaps that much is obvious; for one thing, Seneca said as much nearly two thousand years ago.

The Timepiece

Perhaps you're familiar with the fable of the father who gives a family heirloom watch to his son. "Before I officially hand it over to you," the father tells his son, "please go to the jeweler to find out its worth."

The son does as he is asked and returns disappointed. "The jeweler said it is worth $100, as it is an old model."

"I see," the father replies. "Now try the pawn shop."

The son returns even more dejected. "The pawnbroker offered me only $20."

"Ah," the father says calmly. "Now try the museum in town to see what they say."

The son returns shaking with excitement. "They wanted to give me $250,000 for the watch as it is a precious antique!"

"Now you see," said the father, "never set your own worth by how others value you. Just as with this watch, there will be those to whom you have little value, those to whom you have moderate value, and those who fully appreciate your worth. Spend your time, spend your life, around this last group."

Which is all great advice as far as it goes, but what do you do when the person undervaluing you *is* you? It doesn't matter how much or how little someone else values you if you're incapable and, indeed, unwilling to value yourself accordingly.

That was the position I found myself in as a new entrepreneur. Fortunately, early in my startup career I attended an event at the Georgia State Capitol, where the governor was announcing a new startup program the state was launching, and a chance conversation with another entrepreneur completely changed my thinking.

I was part of a small group of founders mingling prior to the event. Someone came over and struck up a conversation, asking us how things were going with our respective startups. We all responded that things were great, but exhausting. Then the question got to the last person in our group, someone I had not yet met. When asked how things were going with his company, this person answered, "Great. You know, I'm a startup CEO. I barely have anything to do."

I looked over at one of my fellow founders and whispered, "I must be doing this wrong."

The other founder looked at me wide-eyed and responded, "We must all be doing it wrong!"

That is how I met K.P. Reddy, the entrepreneur with an incredible sense of time management. As I got to know him, I learned he is not just a startup founder and CEO, though he is those things many times over. He is also a venture capital investor, now launching his fourth fund. He is also a published author, having written a successful textbook as well as a nonfiction book for entrepreneurs. He is an active mentor to young founders. And he is just getting started.

How is this even possible? How can one human do so much, at such a high level, with such consistency? The answer, I learned, was by assigning the proper value to himself, his time, and most importantly, his mind.

A Penny for Your Thoughts? No Thanks, That Will Be $75 an Hour

Beep. Beep. Beep.

This is why I go to one of the top civil engineering schools in the world and am studying my ass off? K.P. wondered as he diligently steered the forklift.

Sure, this was a part-time job while he was in school, but he knew he had to be worth more than this. And he was, once he graduated: with his degree in hand, K.P. Reddy took a job with a well-known engineering firm and soon was earning a whopping $26,000 a year, much more than he'd made driving a forklift.

But what had once seemed like a sizable raise soon began to feel like peanuts when K.P. saw the bill for his time that went out to a client.

"My employer was billing me at $50 an hour," K.P. recalls. "At $26,000 a year, I was getting only about a quarter of how much they were making off of me. That didn't seem right."

Never one to shy away from questioning things, K.P. approached his manager about the discrepancy.

K.P. says, "He explained that not everyone billed forty hours a week for a full fifty-plus weeks a year, and that besides my salary, my fees had to cover things like benefits, the office space we were in, and other overheads. I asked why he didn't just bill more for my time. His answer was that at my level, with my entry-level skill set, that rate was what the market would bear. In essence, the only way for me to earn more was to work more hours, which I was fine doing."

Work more hours K.P. did, but perhaps not in the way his boss had envisioned. Without realizing it at the time, K.P. internalized advice Epictetus gave millennia before: "You are the one who knows yourself—which is to say, you know how much you are worth in your own estimation, and therefore at what price you will sell yourself; because people sell themselves at different rates." And so, with those extra hours he worked, K.P. chose *not* to sell himself to the firm that was billing him at $50 an hour and only paying him roughly $12.50 of that. Instead, K.P. began putting more time into his side hustle, the website development business he'd started while still in school.

"This was the mid-nineties," K.P. says. "At the time, HTML and JavaScript were scary to people. There weren't a lot of resources out there to teach them what to do, so I helped them."

For his help, clients paid K.P. $75 an hour, and all of that $75 went directly to him, not to some large employer that had to subsidize lower-performing employees or cover a bunch of overhead.

"That's when it clicked for me," says K.P. "Civil engineering is this centuries-old profession. There's a clear path and clear roles, with well-defined value creation, and thus market prices, at each juncture. I really wasn't worth more than $50 an hour to a client or worth more than $12.50 an hour to my employer. The internet, on the other hand, was this totally new thing. My value there was literally six times what it was in civil engineering. It wasn't that my employer was undervaluing me—it was that I wasn't putting my own time to its highest and best use."

The lesson has been one that K.P. has applied throughout his career, and his life, to great effect.

"I learned it was not all about how much I valued my time," he says, "but also about how *others* value it. Something is really only worth what the market is willing to pay. At the same time, I learned that the market itself does not have to be static. In civil engineering, I was like all the other hockey players skating to where the puck was. With website development, I was more like Gretzky skating to where the puck was *going* to be. It made a huge difference."

Over time, K.P. learned that there was even more dynamism in the value equation than he'd initially thought. He had already learned to consider how he valued his time, and he saw how the way others valued that same time depended on the market he was in, and specifically what he was doing in that market. All of this could change. Each hour or minute did not have a static value, but rather had a relative one depending on what else he could be doing at the same time.

K.P. goes on, "There is that saying that if Jeff Bezos walks by a $10,000 bill, he is better off not bending over to pick it up because he makes even more than that each second. That's nonsense. What would he be doing in those specific three seconds that would yield more than the $10,000? The answer is nothing.

"The same is true with how people value their time. They tell themselves, 'I bill at $850 an hour, so that is what my time is worth.' But is it really? What are you doing with that time? Are you billing a client, and so earning $850, or are you just watching TV?"

This aligns with a concept a mentor of mine taught me early in my career. Tom Barkin, then the Chief Risk Officer of the global consulting firm McKinsey & Company (he later became its CFO and then the CEO of the Federal Reserve Bank of Richmond), taught new analysts and associates in McKinsey's southern office about "costly" versus "costless" time.

"Time with my wife and kids," Tom would say, "that is costly. I can't get that back or make up for it elsewhere. Time sitting on an airplane, that is costless time. If I have a set amount of work to do, maximizing the amount of it I complete during that costless time gives me far more of the costly time that I value."

Can Dad Do That?

The somewhat good news is that as a society, we seem to be getting better at this sort of analysis, at least in some areas. While often lamented, the lack of handiness around the house of millennial dads may actually be one such bright spot.

The failure of millennial dads to take on the do-it-yourself (DIY) projects of prior generations is well documented and bemoaned in many quarters. After all, when a third of these dads don't even own a hammer (something 93 percent of their baby boomer predecessors owned),[7] how much can really be expected of them? And this is not just a US phenomenon: across the pond, prior to an uptick during COVID, the United Kingdom's DIY industry was experiencing double-digit annual declines in spending.

So why would I say this is good news? The answer comes down to where these dads seem to be spending their time instead: with their children. In fact, studies show that today's dads are spending on average three times as much time with their children as dads did fifty years ago. That is an astounding uptick, and one that suggests that Tom Barkin is not alone in labeling that time with his family as the "costly" time to be protected.

As K.P. saw with civil engineering, most projects around the house are well defined and have a clear value and cost to complete. At the same time, a professional is likely to be able to do a given project far faster, and cheaper (depending on how you value your time), than an amateur.

This was something I fortunately learned just as my marriage began. My wife and I had just moved into a new home and found that the blinds in our bedroom did a terrible job of blocking the streetlights outside our Midtown Atlanta condo. For several nights in a row, my new bride and I had a very difficult time sleeping. The answer? Blackout curtains.

The problem was that, like so many in my generation, I did not have the right tools, or the knowledge if I am being honest, to properly install the curtains. After a frustrating hour in which I made a mess and accomplished nothing, I called in reinforcements: my dad and my new father-in-law.

Between a pediatric cardiologist (my dad), an entrepreneur and product designer (my father-in-law), and a McKinsey consultant (me), the three of us proceeded to spend the next two hours making an even bigger mess, with no more progress than I had managed on my own. How exactly were we valuing our time?

Once we finally accepted defeat, I called a handyman, who came the following week to install the curtains. Within ten minutes the curtains were up, and the handyman had fixed the mess we had made. While he was there, I asked if he could also fix our garbage disposal, which had been acting up, and he quickly did that as well.

As I went to grab my checkbook, dreading what the total bill would be, I asked over my shoulder, "How much do I owe you?"

"Twenty bucks should do it," the handyman answered.

I turned around, pulled out my wallet, handed over a crisp $20 bill, and promised my new best friend, Dave, that I would never try and do anything around the house myself again and would always call him first—a promise I kept until he moved out of state.

Your Most Important Budget: Where and How to Spend Your Time and Your Mind

All of this raises two important questions: How should you value your own time? And how should you make sure others value you accordingly?

The answer is to take a page from finance. Just as our business or our household develops a budget and then manages it, we need to do the same with our time. But the most effective type of budget is not one that simply tweaks an existing or previous budget, but rather an approach known as "zero-based budgeting." I've adapted this concept and applied it to a method of time valuation I call "zero-based calendaring."

First developed by Peter Pyhrr in the 1970s and made more famous since through its application by numerous successful private equity firms, zero-based budgeting in financial planning is, according to Wikipedia, "a method of budgeting in which all expenses must be justified and approved for each new period." Rather than simply reverting to what has come before as the default starting point, zero-based budgeting forces a clear-eyed assessment of costs and value during each new planning period.

The reason this idea is so useful, and so necessary, when it comes to budgeting and calendaring our own time is that, as we have seen, our value changes. Even within a single period our value can change, depending on what we are doing during any given period and how we, and others, value that time and that activity.

So where should you start in making your own zero-based calendar?

Begin by identifying how and where you want to spend your time in the first place. It's best to start with broad categories like sleep, work, family, eating, exercising, and so on, before diving into the specifics within each.

Once you feel good about your broad categories, the next step is to determine how much time, either on a minute/hourly basis or as a percentage of your week/month/year, you want to allocate to each activity you identified. If your total adds up to more than 168 hours a week, or more than 100 percent depending on your methodology, you will need to go in and do some "time cutting" to rightsize your calendar budget.

Once you've determined the categories and how much time you would like to allocate to each, it's time to map out your ideal week/month/year. In doing this, it's important to both recognize and accept that not every period can or should look exactly the same. There might be weeks when one category takes more than its fair share of your time, and weeks when another does the same to "make up" for those prior weeks. As long as you can acknowledge this going in and not let perfect be the enemy of good, you should still be able to see a more intentional allocation of your time.

The final step in the zero-based calendaring process is to audit your progress as you go—not in retrospect but prospectively. For example, on Friday, look at your calendar for the next week. Does it align with the ideal week you mapped? If not, are there good reasons for this? Should you cancel or rearrange some things to make sure your calendar more closely matches what you wanted? You should do this on a weekly basis, as well as monthly and annually. Use the template at the end of this chapter as a guide.

In doing zero-based calendaring, it's important to remember that this entire process is intended to give you freedom, not shackles. If you find that your initial allocations are getting in your way, the answer is neither to continue to adhere to them unthinkingly nor to throw out the entire concept. Rather, when these times occur, which they will, the answer is to go through the exercise again. More than likely, something has changed—perhaps you have changed how you value your time, perhaps others have changed how they value it, or perhaps you misallocated it the first time around. This is fine. There is no finance team you must get approval from to update your time budget. It's yours. Own it!

Advanced Calendaring for the Busy Professional

As we've already discussed, it's not just how much time we spend working that matters, but what specifically we *do* in that time and how that time is valued by the market. If your goal in a given period of zero-based calendaring is to maximize your market value during that time, then your "work time" bucket will warrant a deeper dive than the other categories.

In these cases, it can actually make sense *not* to start at zero. The first question to ask and answer is "How am I being valued today?" This can be by your employer, by a client, or by someone else, but in any case, it will at least give you a baseline.

With this number in hand, the next question is whether this is a fair market rate. What value are you creating, and is the value others are putting on you commensurate with it? Are there any benchmarks for how others doing similar work are valued? Looking at online job postings for similar roles, or sites like PayScale, can help give you a better sense of this.

All of this helps you determine your value in an as-is state. The exciting part comes when you start thinking through alternative possibilities. What skill sets do you currently possess, or could you build, that would make others value you even more highly? As K.P.'s example demonstrates, this does not have to be an all-or-nothing approach. A totally sensible path could be to work in this higher-value area as a side hustle, as K.P. did, until you can, and want to, make it your main hustle. Past performance is no guarantee of future performance, and past allocations of your time and how others thus value you do not have to lock you into future allocations or fixed values.

Final Sanity Check

Before closing this chapter, I want to recognize that much of the above advice is coldly financial in its approach. The truth is that we each have intangibles that we value as much as, and in many cases even more than, the dollars at stake.

On this point I often think back to how a managing director at McKinsey described the firm. He explained that when it came to purely financial rewards, McKinsey would never be up there with the compensation offered by banks and financial institutions. When it came to pure rewards of the mind, McKinsey would never match academia. And when it came to social impact and purpose, McKinsey would never be on the same level as government service or the nonprofit sector.

"But," the managing director went on to say, "for the kind of person who values all three, there is no better place than McKinsey to optimize across them all."

That others may value things differently really struck home to me in my entrepreneurial career when I hired my first chief technology officer. Trying to hark back to the tripartite structure I learned about from McKinsey, I explained my offer of compensation to the candidate as being across three big buckets: base salary, bonus potential, and equity upside through the stock options that would vest over time.

The candidate nodded and then pointed out that there was actually a fourth bucket that held even more value for him. "Experience," he said. "I've never been a CTO before, and the experience of being one and building out my own technology organization holds its own value for me."

All of this is to say, value doesn't all come down to pure dollars and cents. At my companies, we talk about the enjoyability of the day-to-day at the company: Working on problems that are hard, interesting, and meaningful. Working with people who can, want to, and do help make you better. Working in a way that provides you with the structure to support yourself, and the freedom to allow you to innovate and grow.

All of these things have their own value. The important thing is for you to identify the value *you* place on these intangibles rather than defaulting to the values others may prescribe. After all, if you are going to move from being a tenant of your mind to a masterful owner of it, you want to make sure you are allocating your time and your mind to their highest and best use.

CHAPTER 1 TAKEAWAYS

1. If you don't know your own value, you're leaving money (and mind) on the table.
2. Your value doesn't have to remain static. You can move to higher and better uses, whether that is defined by what the market will pay you for your time or how you personally value it.
3. While financial comparisons can be helpful to a point, life is about much more than money. Identify the intangibles you value, and make sure you are optimizing across these as well.

Zero-Based Calendaring

Area	Desired Allocation (hours or % by week, month, or year)
e.g., sleep, work, family, exercise	

Area	Desired Allocation (hours or % by week, month, or year)

Area	Desired Allocation (hours or % by week, month, or year)
Total (NOTE: If the total is greater than 100 percent of the time available, start cutting!)	

Advanced Mind Budgeting

Current Income	Hours Worked to Earn That	Current Value
		$_____/hour

Price Check (e.g., check open job postings, search on PayScale)

Income on Offer	Hours Expected to Earn That Income	Expected Value
		$_____/hour
		$_____/hour
		$_____/hour
		$_____/hour
		$_____/hour
		$_____/hour
		$_____/hour
		$_____/hour
		$_____/hour

Your Mind's Highest and Best Use

Alternative Uses for Your Time	Market Price/Value for That
	$_____/hour
	$_____/hour
	$_____/hour
	$_____/hour
	$_____/hour
	$_____/hour
	$_____/hour
	$_____/hour

CHAPTER 2

· ·

Surveying Your Boundaries (*Embrace Your Limits*)

To know your value, you must start
by defining the limits of what you
are valuing in the first place.

H ow was your day?" my dad asked as I hopped in the car. A grimace overtook his face as my sweaty body and dirty shoes spoiled the pristine interior of his Chrysler LeBaron convertible. It was Sunday at 5 PM, and I was nine years old. How was my day? On the surface it was great. I had been over at my friend Jared's all afternoon and we had played nonstop for hours. Yet under the surface I'd felt something far different. Even as I was playing soccer, basketball, or video games, or eating a bowl of ice cream to cool off, I'd felt the long shadow of the upcoming week creep over me with ever-greater intensity, darkening my perception of the entire day.

Like many children, and even lots of adults, I was overcome with Sunday dread. Friday after school was amazing, the whole weekend ahead of me. Saturday I was fully immersed in the weekend, and Monday seemed far-off. Sunday morning was great, but by 5 PM? All I could think about was how close Monday was and how far away next weekend suddenly appeared to be. And this particular Sunday was even worse. I had a five-page project I was supposed to turn in on a book about Abraham Lincoln. How the heck was I going to write five whole pages? I hadn't even finished the book.

At that age I had not yet learned the social convention of simply replying "fine" to such a question, so I replied with the openness only a child possesses. "Honestly, Dad," I answered, "my day kind of stunk."

Silence dominated the car until we pulled up to the next red light. "Why?" he asked me, concern creeping into his voice. "What happened at Jared's?"

"Oh, nothing. I mean, it was fun. I just couldn't really enjoy it because all I could think about was this project I have to go home to do now."

My father nodded knowingly and rested a beat before speaking again.

"Don't do that," he told me. "*Never* do that."

"Do what?" I asked.

"Either do the thing you should be doing, or don't do it and don't think about it. But don't *not* do it and then spend the whole time thinking about it! That's the worst. If you're going to obsess about it, you might as well be doing the thing you're putting off. You *will* get it done. You always do. Just make sure you actually enjoy the time you're taking off."

That night I learned that my dad was right: I got the project done, as I always did, and, besides, the bar for a fourth-grade paper isn't really that high to begin with. I finished up the last chapters of my book and cranked out five "brilliant" pages about Honest Abe with spare time to watch a *Saved by the Bell* rerun.

But it wasn't just that Dad's advice was helpful in the moment. His lesson stuck with me for years to come: *Do the thing or don't do it, but don't spend the time you are not doing the thing thinking about it.*

Control Freak

Little did I know that Greek philosopher and Stoic Epictetus addressed the importance and impact of just this sort of control over where we spend our minds two thousand years before my homework was due. "Some things are within our control, and some things are not. It is only after you have faced up to this fundamental rule and learned to distinguish between what you can and can't control that inner tranquility and outer effectiveness become possible." Epictetus's statement is especially powerful considering just how limited things "within his control" were. Epictetus was a former slave. In fact, his name at birth is not even known, and Epictetus in ancient Greek literally means "acquired." In an extreme and literal sense, Epictetus came to realize that even his own body was not in his control. Having lived part of his life according to someone else's will entirely, Epictetus had to learn to define his own "boundaries" within his mind and no further—since the mind is the only thing over which we truly have control. Epictetus applied these insights to his life even after he was set free physically.

Though the Roman emperor Marcus Aurelius lived around the same time as Epictetus, it is hard to imagine a man further removed from Epictetus than he was. Whereas Epictetus's slavery and loss of control over his own body were facts of his existence, surely the most powerful man in the world at the time had no such concerns? And yet, Marcus Aurelius did. Constantly plagued by severe physical pains and maladies, Marcus Aurelius, another famous Stoic, also learned to circumscribe his own boundaries in a limited fashion. In his *Meditations*, he wrote:

> Let the part of your soul that leads and governs be undisturbed
> by the movements in the flesh, whether of pleasure or of pain . . .
> When these affects rise up to the mind by virtue of that other
> sympathy that naturally exists in a body that is all one, then you

must not strive to resist the sensation, for it is natural: but do not let the ruling part of itself add to the sensation the opinion that it is either good or bad.

Marcus Aurelius knew the physical pain was out of his control. But he also recognized that only he could determine what label to put on it. To name the pain was entirely within his control.

As ruler of the most powerful empire of his time, Marcus Aurelius still grasped that the boundary of his own power, though superficially spanning thousands of miles, in fact went no farther than the limits of his mind.

This realization—that nothing but your own mind is within your control—can be an incredibly difficult, limiting, and depressing one, depending on the light in which you look at it. Many of us spend our lives trying to amass power, yet if we consider this honest assessment of our actual "boundaries," we can see that all such power is illusory. We have no more external power after years of work than the power we were born with. At the same time, no matter what anyone does to us, no matter what happens, we have no *less* power than we were born with, either. We all start with mind power. The trouble is, not everyone learns how to exercise it. That's too bad, because it not only affects the quality of life, but can determine one's chances of surviving it.

A Matter of Survival

Nobody knows the essence of mind power better than Commander James Stockdale, former vice admiral in the US Navy and a Medal of Honor recipient. Commander Stockdale was the most senior naval officer held captive during the Vietnam War. When he was locked up as a prisoner of war from 1965 to 1973, he saw and personally experienced innumerable horrors. And while a few prisoners, like him, survived to be released, many more did not.

When asked about which prisoners didn't make it out, Commander Stockdale responded with what has since become known as the Stockdale Paradox:

> Oh, that's easy, the optimists. Oh, they were the ones who said, "We're going to be out by Christmas." And Christmas would come, and Christmas would go. Then they'd say, "We're going to be out by Easter." And Easter would come, and Easter would go. And then Thanksgiving, and then it would be Christmas again. And they died of a broken heart. This is a very important lesson. You must never confuse faith that you will prevail in the end—which you can never afford to lose—with the discipline to confront the most brutal facts of your current reality, whatever they might be.[8]

That's right, the people *least* likely to survive the harrowing experience of a prisoner-of-war camp were those with the most positive thinking. Their optimism about what others might or might not do blinded them to their own mental boundaries.

To put it another way, prisoners of war have no control over when, or if, their captors will release them. By continually setting arbitrary timelines, these poor souls gave their minds to others. In doing so, they gave themselves a false sense of hope and power that was ultimately dashed by the harsh reality that they had no control over their captors, and thus their timelines, whatsoever. Though admitting you have no idea when you will ever see your family and loved ones again could be perceived as a pessimistic outlook, it is also an entirely realistic one in such a situation. It also turned out to be the best recipe for survival.

Viktor Frankl's testimony from even more harrowing circumstances adds another layer of depth to this insight. A concentration camp survivor during the Holocaust, Frankl was also a psychiatrist and is best known for his seminal work *Man's Search for Meaning*.[9] In this book, he describes his own experience as a concentration camp prisoner and the lessons he and other prisoners took away from their experience. In such an extreme situation, the limitations of one's boundaries become abundantly clear.

"Everything can be taken from a man but one thing," writes Frankl, "the last of the human freedoms—to choose one's attitude in any given set of circumstances, to choose one's own way."[10] But whereas Commander Stockdale identified optimism as the death sentence, Frankl saw it differently. Assessing the many deaths he witnessed, whether due to sickness or suicide, Frankl identified "what may have been the real reason for their deaths: giving up hope."[11]

This "hope" may seemingly contradict Commander Stockdale's point about avoiding optimism as a means of survival, but there is nuance here that is important. Frankl was far from optimistic. As he spoke to prisoners about the importance of hope, he also "estimated [his] own chances [of survival] at about one in twenty." He goes on, "But I also told them that, in spite of this, I had no intention of giving up hope. For no man knew what the future would bring, much less the next hour."[12]

My point is that it is not all one or the other: unconditional optimism is not the same as maintaining genuine hope that things may improve. Stockdale and Frankl actually both illustrate the parameters of the boundaries of control. Stockdale knew he could not control what his captors did or did not do, while Frankl knew he could not control what his liberators might or might not do. By setting firm dates that were entirely outside their control, "optimistic" prisoners of war only set themselves up for a harder fall when things did not come to pass as they had envisioned. On the other hand, even as people died around him, even as he objectively assessed his own chances of survival at 5 percent, Frankl recognized the flip side of those same limited boundaries—that things could also get *better*. For Frankl, this was the fuel he needed to stay alive.

This lesson on one's boundaries and their limitations is not just useful in the most extreme life and death situations, but also entirely foundational for taking control of your mind. You can maximize the value of your time and your mind, as K.P. demonstrated, only once you fully understand the circumscribed limits of each. It's only after you objectively assess the boundaries of your mind that you can know where, when, and how to focus that attention. This lesson and this mindset have proved critical in the most extreme instances—from being a slave to ruling an empire, and from being tortured as a prisoner of war to surviving a concentration camp—but they are also incredibly effective when applied in our daily personal and professional lives.

Baker's Billion

For Ed Baker, a serial entrepreneur whose companies have been acquired by FanBridge and Facebook, as well as a former executive of growth at Facebook and Uber and a growth adviser to some of the most promising startups today, knowing what you can control and what you can't is more than a recipe for success—it's a way of life.

"Founding a company is a lot like drilling for oil," Ed explains. "Yes, the best, most experienced companies with the most sophisticated technology can increase their odds of striking oil, but even they cannot guarantee with 100 percent accuracy that any given well will be a success. Intelligence and hard work play a big role, but so does luck."

Whether you are drilling for oil or building a startup, Ed says that, at best, you know the general area that might yield a successful result, but you never know the exact location when you start. Sometimes people get lucky and strike a gusher, and other times very smart and hardworking people come up dry.

Ed sees the same wild variability when it comes to finding "product-market fit," the ultimate metric of success for any startup. "Product/market fit," according to legendary founder and venture capitalist Marc Andreessen, "means being in a good market with a product that can satisfy that market."[13] While this description is perhaps a bit vague, others have put numbers behind the concept, stating that if you've achieved product-market fit, at least 40 percent of your customers would be "very disappointed" if they were to no longer have access to your product.[14]

In order to keep customers, you must first acquire them, and this is where Ed shines. The best and most efficient way to get customers in the door is by "going viral," though in a world that has experienced COVID, the term may have lost some of its shine. The idea of "virality" is that each new customer can actually bring more new customers along with them. If you are able to achieve this in your company, you can grow almost without limit. There are different ways to unearth this virality, but one of the best-known and earliest internet examples was the "Get your free email at Hotmail" link that Hotmail added to the bottom of every single email sent through its service. At a time when many were paying for services like AOL, this link was attributed with helping Hotmail acquire twelve million subscribers over two years with a total investment of $500,000.[15] All of this helped Hotmail sell for $400 million to Microsoft a mere two years after it was founded.

What made Hotmail such a valuable acquisition for Microsoft, however, was not just its viral rate of growth. Even more importantly, Hotmail was great at holding on to those customers it added. To really be successful, you must acquire new customers, *and* you must be able to retain them. This is where the magic of product-market fit comes into play. For all those apps that are successful in driving millions of downloads, the dirty truth is that an estimated 95 percent of apps go unused within three months of being downloaded.[16] No successful business can be built with that kind of falloff.

As an entrepreneur building his own businesses, Ed Baker has found ways to make his products go viral over and over again. With almost unprecedented rapidity, he and his team have been able to drive millions of new users to their products. His first such product was actually a class project. "In that class," he explains, "the professor told us on day one that our final grade would be based upon how many users we could sign up. Five weeks after launch, we went from a single user to five million." In his next venture, Ed was able to get to twenty-five million users before eventually selling to Facebook. In each case, Ed now admits, he and his team were able to drive millions of new users to sign up for their products, but they had a much harder time keeping those users engaged.

Ed attributes many of his later moves to assessing his own boundaries and thus identifying what he could control and what he could not, though in far less dire circumstances than Commander Stockdale or Viktor Frankl. "Finding product-market fit is so hard, and in many ways luck comes into play," Ed says. "I had no control over that. With Facebook and Uber and the companies I am advising now, I was able to go into an environment where it was clear they already had engagement and retention. That has allowed me to focus instead on what I can control and what I do best: growth."

Ed could not control whether or not a product he created would have that desired product-market fit; too much chance came into play for that. Instead, what Ed *could* control was where and how he used his growth-hacking skills. So he chose to apply those skills to companies that had already achieved that desired fit. The results speak for themselves:

When Ed took over international growth for Facebook, it had roughly 500 million users in non-US markets. By the time he left two years later, that number exceeded 1 billion. Essentially, he managed to add as many people to Facebook's platform as lived in the European Union at that time!

The results at Uber were just as striking. When Ed left Facebook to join Uber, it was a relatively little-known ride-sharing company with fewer than 100 million completed trips per year. By the time Ed left the company four years later, that number had climbed to 3.7 billion, a 3,600 percent increase, making the company the most highly valued startup in history.

By parsing out what he could control and what he absolutely could not control, Ed Baker freed up his time and his mind to focus where he in particular was best positioned to exact real, lasting change. By doing this, Ed was valuing himself, and having others value him, at his highest possible rate.

Cool in the Face of Catastrophe

I myself have seen the value and power of identifying and embracing perceived mental boundaries firsthand. Like so many companies and individuals, my company, Rented, was rocked by the COVID-19 pandemic. Operating in the travel industry, a zone that was more negatively affected by the virus than many others, my company faced a great deal of uncertainty. From my employees, my investors, my board members, my customers, and others who were just curious, I continually heard the million-dollar question: "What's going to happen?"

My response was probably not what most were looking for, but that didn't mean it was untrue. Each time someone asked, I explained in the calmest possible voice that there were really three major issues at play:

1. Infection rates
2. Government action in response to those rates (national, state, and/or local)
3. Consumer/traveler response to either and both of the above

Then I hit them with the capper: literally *none* of those things were within our control.

Spending time speculating about what *could* happen would not only have taken mindshare from things that actually were within our control—it would also have set us up for failure, because, if there's one thing that was almost guaranteed to be certain, it was that any speculation I made would undoubtedly be wrong.

Instead, I implored my team members to do the one thing they could: survey their boundaries. If all three of those big, big things were outside their control, then what *was* in their control? Well, the answer was simple: we could control how well we delivered for our clients, how well we communicated with them, how well we listened to their needs, and how well we responded to those needs. If we thought about this in terms of valuing ourselves appropriately, our speculation would be valueless to our clients and to us. Our *actions* for our clients, on the other hand, would hold tremendous value for both.

By identifying our boundaries and remaining laser-focused within them, we achieved astounding results in our business over the course of 2020. Even as travel was being thrashed by COVID-19, we had clients who experienced record years in terms of revenue earned, thanks to the work our team did in quickly launching entirely new products and over-delivering on the customer support we provided every single day. Had we spent our minds worrying about what *might* happen rather than exploring what we could control, we would not have been able to deliver in the same way for our clients. Had we failed to survey our boundaries and instead spent our time trying to control things that we were never going to be able to control, it's doubtful we would have survived at all. By understanding and embracing the boundaries of our control, we instead exited 2020 in an even stronger position than we'd entered it in.

Time to REST

The strength of surveying your boundaries can also be seen as the power of embracing your limits. Rather than wasting time, energy, and mindshare on things outside your control, you need to hunker down and focus on what you can control. In this way, you can truly maximize your personal value, as K.P. already demonstrated in chapter one.

Ed Baker could have spent years working tirelessly and intelligently and still not have hit product-market fit with something he created from scratch. By taking that uncertainty off his plate and working with companies that had already achieved that milestone, he was able to take hold of what he did in fact control and consistently achieve outstanding results.

How can you survey your own boundaries, embrace your limits, and maximize the most of what is in your control?

The answer lies in a simple acronym:

REST: Recognize, Exert, Stop, and Track.

You must first **Recognize** that boundaries exist when it comes to what is within your control and what is not. At a superficial level this may seem obvious, but while you may theoretically Recognize that there are limitations to what you can control, getting to the point where you truly Recognize just *how* limited (and limiting) those boundaries are takes real focused effort—and acceptance.

Take the weather, for example. How often do you complain about it? How much control do you have over it, for good or ill? If you want a different kind of weather, just what are you able to do to get it?

Recognize is the most important element of the REST formula. The world is made up of people who complain about the weather and people who don't. To stop complaining is no small feat—it's the first leap toward achieving a true owner's mindset.

The next step is to **Exert** control where you actually can. This, of course, starts with a singular zone: your mind. In a throwback to the old United Negro College Fund ad, I have to agree that "a mind is a terrible thing to waste." And yet so many of us spend our lives doing just that by not Exerting the control and power we have over our minds. As an exercise, answer the following question: What are you thinking about right now? Don't say "this book," because you know your mind was wandering just a few sentences back. What was it thinking about? What were *you* thinking about? Why did you just give your mind to that thought? You have chosen to invest time in reading this. If there's something stealing that time, find out why and give those nagging thoughts their due. Then get them out of the way.

Which brings us to stage three of the REST formula: after Recognizing your boundaries and Exerting influence on your focus, you must **Stop** spending your mind on those things outside your control. Given that we all do this constantly, just how can we actually Stop?

Begin by reflecting on what has taken up your mind over the past week. What bothered you the most? What excited you the most? What did thinking about those things that bothered or excited you actually *do* for you—did it serve you? What did thinking about those things take away from you? Only you can decide if you are going to spend your mind on those exciting things or those things that bother you. Exert the power you have and Stop wasting your mind where it isn't useful to you.

Now it is time to **Track** how you are doing. As legendary management guru Peter Drucker famously wrote, "What gets measured gets managed." Start measuring *and* managing now by Tracking where you spend your mind. Over the course of the next week, write down where you spent your mind throughout each day—you can use the template at the end of this chapter as your guide. Ideally, you'll want to Track your mind's activity in the moment to get a sense of where you spent your mind and for how long. Then consider: Is this where you want to spend your mind? Is it where you *should* spend your mind? The answers can lead you in profound new directions.

Finally, as you continue to Track, use the "Managing Your Mind" worksheet at the end of this chapter to set targets for the coming day or week—goals for how you'd like to spend your mind. These targets will do two magical things: First, they will give you an honest assessment of just how successfully you are staying within your mental boundaries. Second, over time, these targets and your results will better equip you to distinguish what you can and can't control. If you do this, no longer wasting your mind on things you cannot control, and instead focusing your time and attention on only those things you can, you will achieve "that inner tranquility and outer effectiveness" Epictetus wrote about so long ago.

CHAPTER 2 TAKEAWAYS
. . . .

1. Exercising meaningful control over your mind starts with understanding, and indeed accepting, the limited boundaries of that control.

2. Nobody can force you to spend your mind on something. Only you can do that. You can choose to give away this superpower or fully embrace it yourself.

3. In order to set and maintain your own boundaries, you must first **REST**.

    a. **Recognize** what is in your control and what isn't.

    b. **Exert** control where you actually can.

    c. **Stop** spending your mind on areas you have no control over.

    d. **Track** your progress in developing this key skill.

Tracking Your Mind

Time	What You Were Doing	What You Were Thinking About
6–7 AM		
7–8 AM		
8–9 AM		
9–10 AM		
10–11 AM		
11 AM–12 PM		
12–1 PM		
1–2 PM		
2–3 PM		
3–4 PM		

4–5 PM		
5–6 PM		
6–7 PM		
7–8 PM		
8–9 PM		
9–10 PM		

Managing Your Mind

Area	Desired Allocation (% of day, week, etc.)*	Actual Allocation (%)
e.g., work, family, friends		

---

* You can refer back to the exercise you completed in chapter one as a starting point.

CHAPTER 3

· ·

Thank You, Sir, May I Have Another? (*The Gift of Criticism*)

> Setting your boundaries and knowing your
> value enables you to decide when and how
> to rent to others for the greatest effect.

What are you working on these days?"

This might have been nothing more than polite small talk, but whatever motivated the question, the person asking had no way of knowing just how excited I was to answer it.

"I actually just started a new company," I gushed. "It's going really well so far."

"Really?"

Maybe I was reading too much into the raised eyebrow—had my friend Keith changed his tone all of a sudden? Maybe the surprise I thought I heard was directed at the idea that *anyone*, not just me in particular, would have the audacity to start a company. Maybe.

"What does your company do?"

Now he was in for it. Everyone's favorite subject is themselves—everyone except for new founders. Their favorite subject is their company.

"It securitizes the vacation rental market."

In retrospect, the glazed-over look should have told me that Keith was no longer picking up what I was putting down, but nothing could stop me now that I had started.

"You know how Airbnb and Vrbo are marketplaces for people to book a night or a week at a time in a vacation home?" I asked.

I did not wait for an answer before continuing.

"My company is like that, but for a year at a time. Instead of renting to a guest, the homeowner puts all of the weeks they want to rent in the following year into a single block, and local management companies bid against one another to buy that whole block. Once the manager has the block, they can break it into a night or a week at a time and rent it on Airbnb and Vrbo. The homeowner gets a guaranteed income stream, and the professional manager gets a new property to manage with the potential to make more money than they paid for the right to rent it."

I finally stopped to breathe and to smile broadly. Anyone watching could be forgiven for thinking I was standing there waiting for a round of applause for my virtuoso performance.

"I see," said Keith finally. "Are there any companies out there that are already doing this?"

Was he implying that I wasn't smart enough to come up with an original idea? Was he suggesting that surely hundreds of others had already beaten me to the punch?

"No!" I answered proudly. "Every manager works on commission today, and owners are getting tired of it. That's why so many are switching to Airbnb and Vrbo to do the property management themselves."

"If they are all on commission today," Keith asked me, "then why would they want to take all of this financial risk by instead guaranteeing a fixed amount to the homeowner?"

OK. So my idea, which just moments before was so obvious that tons of others must already be doing it, was now such a bad idea that no one would ever do it? I had my response ready without having to think about it.

"Two reasons," I responded. "The first is that the best managers, the ones who can make the most from a home, are going to make more from doing it this way than the old commission way. And most homeowners are happy to take a significant discount to get a guaranteed income stream."

"And the other reason?" Keith asked me.

"They won't have a choice," I answered proudly. "Once all the owners demand this model as the only way they will work with a manager, no one will be able to stay in business without doing it this way."

"Then why do you think no one has done this yet?" Keith asked.

I see you, Keith, and I see your jealousy. I see you trying to break down my idea, and me. Surely, I couldn't possibly be smart enough to come up with something original that is also good.

"The market wasn't right until now." I regurgitated my canned response. "Before the online booking sites took off, owners had no option but to go to a manager working on commission. Now that the homeowners can rent their properties themselves on these sites, they are leaving managers in droves. The managers are desperate to convince owners to work with them. Owners have more power now, and my company helps them unlock it."

I finished with a note of finality. What had been my favorite topic of conversation minutes before didn't seem quite so fun or interesting to me any longer. The conversation drifted on to the fall weather and that year's football season. And maybe that's what Keith had been hoping for all along.

It Is Not the Critic Who Counts

In your own life, you have likely dealt with your fair share of critics. To do anything of any real importance or meaning inevitably attracts them. Some of these critics will be driven by jealousy, some will be driven by fear, and some may seemingly just be incapable of doing anything but tear other people down.

In your own life, you might do as I did with Keith and many others in those early days of my first company: erect defensive walls against your critics, not wanting to let them get in the way of your dreams and ambitions. And indeed, this is what we are often taught to do. Probably the single most famous quote about critics is from President Theodore Roosevelt's "Man in the Arena" speech:

> It is not the critic who counts; not the man who points out how the strong man stumbles, or where the doer of deeds could have done them better. The credit belongs to the man who is actually in the arena, whose face is marred by dust and sweat and blood; who strives valiantly; who errs, who comes short again and again, because there is no effort without error and shortcoming; but who does actually strive to do the deeds; . . . and who at the worst, if he fails, at least fails while daring greatly, so that his place shall never be with those cold and timid souls who neither know victory nor defeat.

The modern-day philosopher Jay-Z expresses the sentiment more succinctly: "Fuck critics, you can kiss my whole asshole! If you don't like my lyrics, you can press fast forward."[17]

And yet, if we take this approach with our critics, which I clearly did for quite a while, we are missing out on an opportunity. We are failing to accept a gift. Yes, a gift. As Marcus Aurelius wrote in his *Meditations*,

"If anyone can refute me—show me I'm making a mistake or looking at things from the wrong perspective—I'll gladly change. It's the truth I'm after, and the truth never harmed anyone. What harms us is to persist in self-deceit and ignorance."

Too often, I treated conversations like mine with Keith as a battle of wits. I erected barriers preventing anyone from breaking into my head-space, even when what they were offering could have been beneficial. I was identifying what I perceived to be my boundaries, but in doing so I erected impenetrable walls when the better answer was to instead build gates with doors that could allow in invited guests and their potentially constructive feedback. Rather than trying to uncover the truth, which might have helped me see the limitations of my eventually shuttered startup before I invested years and untold sums into it, I wanted to prove I was right. I wanted to win the argument, not get to a better answer. This limited my learning, and thus limited what I could and did bring to my company. I spent my time searching for evidence that I was right rather than evidence to the contrary, even when people were doing their utmost to serve me the latter on a silver platter. It turned out that my original idea was not a bad one. It actually worked. It just was not nearly as big of an idea as I deluded myself into believing.

Listening to the critics—truly hearing what they have to say—doesn't have to mean I take every statement as pure fact, saddling myself with overwhelming self-doubt. It does not have to mean that I mindlessly hand my mind over to them and again relegate myself to being a mental tenant. I found another, better option. As the owner of my mind, I can decide when and how to open the gates around it. I can proactively choose how and when I rent my mind to others, ultimately expanding those boundaries and my own potential through learning and growth.

Had I more fully engaged with my critics and learned from what they were offering me, I might have seen a better answer before it was too late. This is true of my interaction with Keith, but the truth is, it is just one example of many similar conversations I had at that time. Had I appreciated my critics' insights more fully, I might have been able to more effectively identify my own boundaries and those of my company—and recognize that they were different than I'd originally imagined. Perhaps, instead of working so hard to prove the critics wrong, I could have focused my time and my mind where they would have achieved a more successful result.

Very Well Then I Contradict Myself (I Am Large, I Contain Multitudes)

I'm not alone in my seeming allergy to criticism. In fact, it's so common that it has a name: confirmation bias. Wikipedia defines confirmation bias as "the tendency to search for, interpret, favor, and recall information in a way that confirms or supports one's prior beliefs or values." Think about it: When you get into an argument with someone and want to prove you're right, what does your Google search look like? Is it truly open-ended, seeking out the truth, or is it highly targeted to yield the evidence that will support your point of view so you can "win" the argument?

But what is "winning" in this context? In a conversation with a critic, what can you be said to have won? If you are actually wrong and the person trying to help you see that gives up, who ultimately loses the most in that encounter? We value consistency, often at the cost of correctness. We have an innate fear of being seen as "flip-floppers." We've even seen this label spell doom for aspiring politicians.

The Stoics would argue that we should take the exact opposite approach to prioritizing consistency over the truth. Consistency is not helpful, and is indeed harmful, if you are consistently wrong. To stubbornly insist on remaining "consistent," even when presented with evidence to the contrary, is to hand the current ownership of your mind over to your prior, wrong way of thinking. This is not just theoretical. It can and often does have a real and human cost—just think of how many mothers' lives were needlessly lost because for years doctors refused to accept that their unwashed hands were to blame for high maternal mortality even when presented with the evidence.[18] The only way to correct such wrongs is to be open to criticism, whether it comes from someone else or from yourself. As the economist John Maynard Keynes is famously reported to have said when he was accused of flip-flopping, "When my information changes, I change my mind. What do you do?"

· · · · · ·

One incredible example of flip-flopping when faced with the truth comes from Supreme Court Justice John Marshall Harlan. Justice Harlan is perhaps most famous for being the lone dissenting voice in *Plessy v. Ferguson* in 1896. As a reminder, the *Plessy* decision created the doctrine of "separate but equal" races that would plague American society and perpetuate segregation for more than half a century after the ruling. Not surprisingly, this decision, along with the *Dred Scott* decision of 1857 that upheld slavery even in the free states, is perennially on the short list of "worst Supreme Court decisions of all time."

In contradiction to his colleagues, who believed "the white race . . . to be the dominant race," Justice Harlan argued, "In the view of the Constitution, in the eye of the law, there is in this country no superior, dominant, ruling class of citizens. There is no caste here. Our Constitution is color-blind and neither knows nor tolerates classes among citizens. In respect of civil rights, all citizens are equal before the law."[19] From the perspective of our own time, his argument seems not only obvious and right, but also the only morally correct one in this situation. And yet, even more remarkable than how right Justice Harlan was in the eyes of history when everyone else he worked with was so wrong, was the journey that the justice took to get there.

John Marshall Harlan, you see, was a Kentuckian from a slaveholding and slavery-defending family. In the years prior to the *Plessy* decision, he had advocated not only for the "superiority of the white race" but indeed for the legality and morality of slavery. But as Justice Harlan witnessed violent attacks on African Americans during Reconstruction, he changed, he learned, and he grew as a person. With greater age, experience, and wisdom, Harlan later said, "I have lived long enough to feel and declare that . . . the most perfect despotism that ever existed on this earth was the institution of African slavery . . . With slavery it was death or tribute . . . It knew no compromise, it tolerated no middle course. I rejoice that it is gone." Unsurprisingly, he too was labeled a flip-flopper, a label he embraced. "Let it be said that I am right rather than consistent," he declared.[20]

It would have been easy—far easier, in fact—for Justice Harlan to seek out those who agreed with his starting position. His family, his neighbors, his political party, and indeed his fellow justices on the Supreme Court would have been all too ready to confirm Harlan's initially held beliefs as correct. How easy it would have been to perceive the critics of these same beliefs as enemies he should argue and fight against. Harlan sought not, however, to confirm what he already thought he knew. Rather, Harlan spent his life seeking out the truth—not only when it strengthened the argument of his critics, but *especially* when it did so. More than one hundred years after his passing, it is impossible to argue against the fact that this pursuit of truth ultimately led Harlan to the "right" answer on perhaps the most critical question of his time.

So how is one to balance conviction with the gift of criticism? How do you avoid being dissuaded by unhelpful or malicious critics, while still being strengthened by the gift of the criticism on offer? To say we should not be renters of our own minds is not to say that we should never open or rent our mind to others. Indeed, one of the greatest powers that mind ownership unlocks is the very ability to determine how, when, to whom, and for what "price" we will rent our mind in order to achieve the greatest effect. Knowing how and when to receive, synthesize, and act upon criticism is one of the best illustrations of this power at work.

Making Criticism Count

Kat Cole has made a career of using criticism to her advantage and advancement. She began as a hostess at her local Hooters in Jacksonville, Florida, and eventually worked her way up to running an entire conglomerate of restaurants that included brands like Moe's Southwest Grill, Jamba Juice, and Cinnabon in her role as the president and COO of Focus Brands. Along the way, Kat credits her precipitous climb to her ability and desire to seek out criticism.

"When I turned eighteen," Kat shares, "I moved from being a hostess to a server. Let me tell you, if you want quick and frequent criticism, there is nothing better than the restaurant industry."

Kat learned that many servers would just walk away after dropping off food to dine-in patrons, creating problems down the line when things did not turn out as expected. Instead, Kat says she became well trained in the art of "two bites or two minutes." This meant that she would check back in with the table either after the diners had consumed two bites of what she had dropped off or after two minutes had passed. The reason is that although most servers ask, "Do you have everything?" when they first set a plate down, most diners do not actually know yet. They just default to saying yes. If the server leaves and doesn't circle back within two bites or two minutes, any issues the diners may experience can frustrate them and ultimately affect the server's tip.

"Pretty soon," Kat continues, "I learned it wasn't enough to wait for diners to ask. I learned how to be more proactive with my questions, rather than just reactive two minutes or two bites later. When I would first bring the food, I would ask, 'Do you want more ketchup? Would you like an extra bowl for the bones from your wings?' Things like that. The people at the table may only eat there once a month, and not know what they need. I served scores of tables just like them every single day. I could anticipate their needs before they realized they had them."

This proactivity, in turn, made Kat a more efficient server, creating more downtime, and thus even more time to be proactive.

"I remember one day that was kind of slow," Kat shares. "One of my tables had ordered a bucket of oysters, so when I brought the bucket to the table, I also brought my glove and offered to shuck some for them. They were blown away."

The tip they left also blew Kat away. She quickly learned that when there was the time, helping people shuck their oysters, or even cracking their snow crab legs for them,* had some interesting downstream effects. For one, it impressed the diners. Additionally, since neither oysters nor crab legs are too filling, Kat learned that if she sped up the process, people then consumed what she brought to their table that much faster. And since they usually weren't full, they then tended to order even more. The total bill ended up being bigger, and this, compounded by how impressed they often were with Kat's assistance, led her tables to leave ever-larger tips.

Around the time she turned nineteen, Kat's role changed once again. In addition to working as a server, she was also sent around the world to open new Hooters locations. After serving on the team that launched new

---

* Kat got to where she could crack one pound of crab legs in a minute flat.

Hooters in Australia and then Orlando, Kat led the team that launched Hooters in Nassau in the Bahamas, as well as in Argentina. It was while she was in South America that she received a lesson in criticism that she has heeded ever since.

"The idea with a franchise business," Kat explains, "is that there is this commonality between each and every location. At the same time, to be successful in new markets, we had to adapt to local tastes. Opening in Argentina was definitely a wake-up call."

That call initially came from the cooks she was training for the new restaurant to open in Buenos Aires.

"I remember, we had set up the kitchen and gotten all the supplies in, and we were training the cooks on the items on the menu when there was this total revolt," Kat explains. "I speak Spanish, so I soon understood that they found our quality of meat unacceptable. 'This is the beef capital of the world,' they said to me 'You cannot serve this *mierda* to Argentinians.'"

Kat heard them out. Switching ingredients was not impossible or unheard of.

"'We can order better steak,'" I told them. "But they weren't satisfied. 'That won't do,' they told me. 'You cannot cook a proper steak on these flattop grills. We need a *real* flame.' Now I was worried," says Kat. "The franchise owner had just purchased all of this equipment *we* told him to buy, and now I was going to have to go to him and tell him not only that it was unusable, but that he was going to have to go buy even more new equipment? I was definitely worried about how he would take it."

Worried but not deterred, Kat scheduled a meeting with the franchise owner to set out the problems, as well as the recommended solution she had worked out with the team back in HQ. And it was in that meeting that she received the advice she says she will never forget.

The new franchise owner was not happy, as was expected, but he agreed with the reasoning and the plan Kat had put together. Before they parted, he shared some advice with her.

"When you get criticized," he said, "first assume it's correct. Then you will be prepared to respond and address it. Otherwise, you waste your time debating the merits."

He went on. "More often than not, there is a grain of truth to any criticism. If you don't get caught up in the back-and-forth, you are more likely to identify and understand that grain of truth and to immediately identify a solution."

"I have carried his advice with me through my entire career," Kat says now. "It's this humility to accept that I can be criticized, and this courage to then act on it."

Starting in a restaurant where there are multiple and immediate feedback loops throughout every shift, along with receiving such profound advice early on, helped make Kat not just comfortable with criticism, but in many ways also hooked on it. Which is what made Kat's next move, this time into corporate, so difficult.

"When you are physically working *in* the restaurant," Kat says, "the feedback loop is pretty instantaneous. You can see it on someone's face as soon as you put the order on the table. In corporate, there are maybe quarterly review cycles. I found it so difficult to tell how I was doing and to learn how to keep improving."

Difficult, but not impossible. While Kat no longer sat in the restaurant in her day-to-day work, she found that the fact that she had so recently come from that environment also made her more likely than her peers to seek feedback, and even criticism. She was able to control how she went about seeking input from the field, input she knew held great value.

"If I was developing a new menu, or procedure, or training manual," Kat explains, "early in that process I would take it to real restaurants to test. To hear and see how people in the restaurant reacted and responded."

Kat still carries this hunger to seek out real and relevant feedback today.

"It took a lot of time," Kat admits. "The shift initially to corporate was so abrupt. I finished serving in a restaurant on a Saturday night, and Monday I was in the office. In shift work, the work *is* the feedback. As I moved into corporate I had to be more intentional about seeking out that feedback and about physically going out myself to get it. It's a lot of work, but it's definitely been worth it."

TRIED and True

All too often, we are uncomfortable with criticism. Scared of it, even. And yet, it is inevitable. "If you absolutely can't tolerate critics, then don't do anything new or interesting," Jeff Bezos has said. Who would willingly resign themselves to a life like that? Certainly not you.

However, getting comfortable with criticism is one thing. Actively seeking it out, as Kat Cole has done throughout her career, is going to the next level. But her example also demonstrates that even that is not enough. You must also *do* something with it. As a client of mine once told me, "It's not just that you and your team ask for my input; almost everyone does that. What I love about you guys is that you *act* on it. You have no idea how rare that is." Rare becomes noticed, and noticed becomes appreciated.

Which is why I have found the following framework to be so effective when it comes to accepting, processing, and acting on criticism. I call it:

TRIED and True: Take time, Reflect,
Identify, Echo, then Deliver.

Let's take each step in turn.

The first thing to do when you receive criticism is to **Take time**. More often than not, when we receive criticism, our defensive walls go up. Rather than seeking to understand or improve from the criticism offered, our default is to reject it in defending our own position. This may be a natural starting point, but it does not have to remain our ending point. By taking time after receiving the criticism, you can allow your default reactions to calm, and put yourself in a better position to see and accept the gift on offer.

With the extra time, the next step is to **Reflect** on what you heard. What did the person actually say? How was the criticism intended? What was *not* said? All of this is informative as you move to the next step in the process.

Through this reflection, you are now ready for the third step: to **Iden- tify** what in this criticism is worth addressing and what is not. Just as Kat learned, any criticism comes with at least a grain of truth. Even when you don't want to hear it, with Time and Reflection, can you Identify that helpful and useful grain in this particular situation? This is the crucial filter in determining what, and how much, of your mind and your time to rent to the critic and their criticism.

This brings us to the fourth step, wherein you **Echo** back to the critic what you believe you heard. This will allow you to focus on the grain of truth you identified as relevant, and thus gather additional information, details, or instructions that will be helpful as you move to the last step.

The fifth and final step is to **Deliver**. Accepting criticism is one thing. Processing and synthesizing, and even playing it back to the critic, is yet another. But still, the real magic, the true unwrapping of the gift that criticism can be, does not come until you act upon it and actually Deliver the necessary changes, thus making the most of what you got from the grain (or more) of truth that was offered to you by the critic.

This process of using criticism to your advantage is not always easy, and it does take time. The more you do it, however, the more it will become second nature, replacing the defensive walls that are all too often the barriers preventing us from the growth we seek. As K.P. and Ed demonstrated in chapters one and two, respectively, identifying our value and our boundaries is invaluable. However, as Kat's story also shows, creating unnecessarily rigid boundaries and barriers holds us back from becoming better, and even more valuable, versions of ourselves.

CHAPTER 3 TAKEAWAYS
. . . .

1. Critics, to steal a phrase from elsewhere, "you will always have with you."
2. While it is important not to be held back by critics, it is also important not to hold yourself back from the growth the critics can help you achieve.
3. To make the most of the gift on offer, there is a **TRIED and True** framework you can use:
    a. **Take time** after receiving the feedback to process.
    b. **Reflect** on what you heard—and think you heard.
    c. **Identify** the "grain of truth" in the criticism that is worth acting on.
    d. **Echo** back to the critic what you think you heard to get additional detail and clarification.
    e. **Deliver** on the changes necessary.

TRIED and True Worksheet

Take Time
When did you receive the feedback? Have your natural walls of defense gone down?

Reflect
Break down what the critic said into individual components:

- Was there anything they praised?

- What *specifically* did they criticize?

- Why would this seem true to them? Look at things from their perspective.

Identify
What grain or grains of truth are there?

Echo
Script how to play back to the critic what you believe you heard, focusing on the grains of truth.
What edits or clarifications did they provide?

Deliver
Get to work!

PART II
. . . .
Mind Renting and Circumstances and Events

CHAPTER 4

. . . .

When It Is the Best of Times, Get Ready for the Worst of Times (*Prepare Ahead of Time*)

Prepare yourself for when things inevitably go wrong by playing out the worst-case scenarios ahead of time.

As common and harmful as it is for us to hand over our minds to other people, even more prevalent and more difficult to overcome is our tendency to give our minds to something less tangible: events and circumstances that are outside our control. If other people are definitionally beyond our boundaries, as we have seen, then how much more so are events that involve more than one person, like electoral politics, or circumstances beyond the control of humans entirely, such as the weather? And yet, despite our impotence in controlling these events and circumstances, most of us settle, intentionally or not, for renting the remnants of our minds to these outside forces, whether it's by engaging in social media shouting matches, incessantly scrolling for 24/7 news updates, or allowing our mood to be dictated by the outcome of a sporting event. It doesn't have to be this way, as I have slowly and painfully learned.

· · · · · ·

I was half a decade into my entrepreneurial journey and could barely keep my eyes open. Somehow, exhausted as I was, sleep had not come for the last three nights. I felt like a zombie walking into the office and could barely stay focused, even when I was supposed to be the one leading a meeting or conversation. That morning I had once again completely spaced out as I drove my daughter to school, realizing she was talking to me only after she shouted "Daddy!" at me who knows how many times in a row. Sure, I had a philosophy on paper and knew how I *wanted* to live my life in theory, but every aspect of my life I was failing to actually live it in practice.

What had sent me down this negative spiral? My business was on the brink of collapse. Prospects that had looked promising months before had suddenly turned to a nightmare scenario as some of the "surefire" bets we had made (or I had made) turned sour very quickly. The company's cash position was rapidly deteriorating, and its existing investors were losing patience. Everything I had worked so hard to build was crashing down around me, and it was all my fault.

Even though I was an avid student of Stoicism, I had completely failed to follow Seneca's advice to Lucilius:

> If an evil has been pondered beforehand, the blow is gentle when
> it comes. To the fool, however, and to him who trusts in fortune,
> each event as it arrives "comes in a new and sudden form," and
> a large part of evil, to the inexperienced, consists in its novelty.

This is proved by the fact that men endure with greater courage, when they have once become accustomed to them, the things which they had at first regarded as hardships. Hence, the wise man accustoms himself to coming trouble, lightening by long reflection the evils which others lighten by long endurance.

Seneca was right; I had been a fool. This "new and sudden" event I was experiencing was certainly novel, and it wasn't the good kind of novelty. Had I been wiser, I would have accustomed myself to the potential trouble before it ever came about. That I had failed to do so was now biting me, and my entire company, firmly in the ass.

However, what kept me up at night, and what felt like a heavy blanket of dread hanging over me all day, was not what had already happened. Or rather, it wasn't *just* what had already happened. What I was now most anxious about, and was giving ownership of my mind to night and day, was what *could* happen going forward.

Understanding this, I also realized that just because I failed to heed Seneca's advice once did not mean I could not still benefit from it. I had plenty of fear about the future, but at that time it was still ill-defined. Now was the time to get more precise. What was it that I actually feared?

So often we are told *not* to be pessimistic. We are instructed to hope for the best. We are told that the "law of attraction" will mean that our thoughts, positive or negative, will bring about correlating positive or negative events in our lives. Not only is this wrong, but it can also be downright dangerous, as Commander Stockdale's story, in which "positive thinking" became deluded optimism, demonstrated in chapter two.

Of course, the Stoics also realized this. Seneca knew that blind optimism, whereby we literally are unable and unwilling to envision the downside possibilities, puts us in a position where we are unable to prepare for them or prevent them from occurring in the first place. Rather than be like an ostrich with our head in the sand, pretending nothing bad can ever happen, we are far better served by playing out the worst case, the *real worst case*, and then asking ourselves, "Is this really so bad?"

So that is just what I did—I forced myself to consider the worst case. I mean, the really worst thing that could happen given the death spiral my company seemed to be in. My first analysis imagined that the worst thing that could happen would be a "down round." This would mean we would still get an investment to keep the company going, but at a valuation lower than the one we'd previously raised, significantly decreasing the personal economics for all existing shareholders.

I soon realized, however, that I was being too soft on myself and on my company. That was not the worst case. The worst case would be if we received no investment at all. If that happened, we could soon find ourselves bankrupt, and all of our employees would be jobless, myself included. Great, mission accomplished! I had now done the first step and imagined the truly *worst* case possible. The next step was to reflect on this imagined reality as a thought experiment. With my company shuttered, what would happen then?

Besides the hit to my ego of having steered the company I founded into the metaphorical iceberg, I soon found that the worst case was not actually all that bad. At the time, I was being paid less than a quarter of what I'd made prior to founding the company, and I was constantly pushing off headhunters who were offering me new positions that were far more lucrative than the one I would be losing. Likewise, every single one of my employees had taken pretty significant pay cuts in order to work at the company. The actual worst case, then, would be that everyone would end up elsewhere in pretty short order, making more money each month than they were making at present. Is this the condition that I feared so much?

To say I slept well that night would be an understatement. Having been sleep deprived for much of the preceding week, I went down like a log, and for what may have been the first time on a weekday, my daughter had to wake me up. Once I was well rested and the fog in my mind had cleared, I was in a far better position to steer my company out of the mess. Before too long, we managed to exit the loss-making lines of business and to line up a new round of investment that positioned us to succeed for years to come. As the Stoics would have known, it was actually the law of *inverse* attraction that helped me achieve positive results from my negative thinking.

The Super Worst Case

One consistent problem with electoral politics is that politicians on a two-, four-, or even six-year election cycle have little reason to think of the long term. With voters no doubt asking them, "What have you done for me lately?" they attach far more importance to immediate and visible actions and results. So perhaps it should not have been surprising that after years of underinvestment, a January 2018 audit of Atlanta's IT infrastructure commissioned by its newly elected mayor, Keisha Lance Bottoms, found between 1,500 and 2,000 vulnerabilities that left the city's systems open to attack. However, even with this knowledge in hand, the city could not fix the problem overnight.

And so even as the new administration was trying to get things into a better position, disaster struck. Hackers exploited the city's vulnerabilities and successfully executed a ransomware attack that crippled the Atlanta city government's ability to conduct business online. City employees and residents had to resort to filling in forms by hand and paying bills in person for weeks. The full extent of the damage from the attack was not even known for months, but given Atlanta's national importance as an economic and transportation hub, the attack and fallout garnered a lot of international attention, putting my city in the spotlight for all the wrong reasons.

Few people would willingly walk into a situation like this. Even fewer would accept a leadership position and the responsibility for getting things in order for the long term, given the dire state at the time. But Gary Brantley is not like other people. Having already spent more than a decade and a half as a public servant and chief information officer of two different school districts, Gary saw his city in need and he ran to the fire—not away from it. And so, in October 2018, about six months after the attack, Gary took over as the commissioner and chief information officer for the city of Atlanta. The bad news was that he had quite the mess to clean up. The even more daunting news was that if Atlanta had already been in the spotlight, it was about to *become* the spotlight, because in a few short months the city was set to host the most watched event in the United States: Super Bowl LIII. The city's new commissioner and CIO, and the author of *The Art of Organization Transformation*, was up for the challenge.

"For months leading up to the Super Bowl," Gary shares, "we started conducting tabletop exercises.[*] In these we would run through *all* the things that could happen and go wrong, and exactly how we would respond in each."

Though the responsibility rested firmly on Gary's shoulders, the exercises involved far more than just his team, or even just city officials.

"We had people involved from the city, state, and federal levels," Gary says, "as well as from the private sector like [the public utility provider] Southern Company, Delta, Coca-Cola, Home Depot, and UPS. All told, we had 135 people in the room, and each person was chosen because of

---

[*] Ready.gov defines tabletop exercises as "discussion-based sessions where team members meet in an informal, classroom setting to discuss their roles during an emergency and their responses to a particular emergency situation. A facilitator guides participants through a discussion of one or more scenarios." See https://www.ready.gov/exercises.

their experience and responsibility for security and emergency response in their organization."

Even though Gary's mandate, on its face, was solely virtual, the exercises by necessity covered not just the digital systems of the city but also its physical infrastructure.

"It was all these things you probably wouldn't think about," Gary says. "For example, we had to secure the physical perimeter for the venue, and so had to think about all of the ways that could be jeopardized. This meant that even though the Super Bowl was not until February, I had to put out an executive order stopping all digging and construction within a certain radius of the stadium as early as November."

"We had to push every system to its limit," Gary goes on. "We had to shut down the power in the stadium to see if, and for how long, it could really run on its solar power alone."

This was not an idle concern, as anyone who watched Super Bowl XLVII go completely dark in New Orleans just a few years earlier can attest.

"We had to see if we could hack into the communication systems," Gary continues, "and we could. We had to develop a plan for how we would respond if that happened. I mean, think about it, there are few things likely to cause more of a panic than a hacker taking over the scoreboard and telling everyone he's about to set off a bomb in the stadium."

And it wasn't just the stadium and the surrounding environs that were potentially at risk. From the power grid to the water system, from vehicular traffic on the city's streets to human traffic in what was already the world's busiest airport, every area, from the grandest scale to the most minute, had to be considered, analyzed, tested, and planned for.

"If you're not personally in it," Gary admits, "it might seem overboard. But just look at the Super Bowl in Tampa. The Friday before, a hacker got into their water system and poisoned the city's water supply. The risks are real!"

Running through the scenarios and testing systems, however, was just the start.

"It wasn't enough to just run through this stuff on paper. We had to actually live it. Even the response after the fact. When crisis hits, you don't want that to be the first time you're dusting off the playbook. You want to have built the muscle memory of how you're going to respond and what you're going to say."

This is why the tabletop exercises also included dress rehearsals of who would respond to each crisis, what they would say, and when and how they would communicate to the public. The upshot was that the Super Bowl was a success for the city (and, as a bonus, helped it move past the epic collapse of its home team, the Falcons, two years prior). But the exercises and their lessons didn't stop there.

"This isn't all for a single event," Gary explains. "As a government, as an organization, this just has to become a way of operating."

With Gary in the city's leadership, it did become the standard way of operating, and has remained so. This is one reason why, even as the city was dealing with protests and looting after an Atlanta police officer tragically shot and killed Rayshard Brooks at a local Wendy's in June 2020, at the height of a nationwide backlash against police violence and racial inequality, the profile of Atlanta's mayor actually rose; at one point, she was even on the shortlist of potential vice presidential running mates for Joe Biden.

"She was ready for that," Gary shares. "That was something she had practiced, something she rehearsed. When a lot of other cities and mayors were trying to figure things out, Mayor Bottoms was able to rely on her muscle memory. In essence, she rose to the occasion by falling back on her training."

These lessons and practices are not just limited to the high-profile public sector. Having helped get his city back on track, Gary has since moved on to the private sector, now serving as the chief technology officer of one of the largest home development companies in the country.

"We aren't going to be able to stop every bad thing from happening," Gary reflects. "But as a leader, I can help make sure we're ready for them and know what to do when they do occur. A lot of people are scared of thinking through the worst-case scenario. The thing is that if you don't, that worst case can be even worse. You have to get ahead of it."

Hell Week

Depending on your particular job, a "bad day at the office" could mean any number of things. Your boss could have been especially jerky that day, your coworker's unreliability might have left you in a bind, your client could have been exceptionally demanding and ungrateful—the possibilities and the "badness" levels of the day can vary widely. That said, there are very few of us whose bad day at the office comes even close to comparing to an average day at work for a Navy SEAL. Thinking about how extraordinary a SEAL's "ordinary" is can give us some perspective on just how problematic, and indeed dangerous, their "worst cases" can be.

This is why so much of a SEAL's assessment, selection, and training is built around the ability to prepare for and adapt to these worst-case scenarios.

"Our job," says Rich Diviney, "is to prepare for the worst. For us, the worst is always uncertainty."

As a retired Navy SEAL commander who was formerly in charge of assessment, selection, and training for a specialized and elite unit within the already specialized and elite Navy SEALs, Rich knows what he's talking about.

"Uncertainty is so dangerous," Rich explains, "because when we are faced with it, our natural response is to have our sympathetic nervous system take over."

The sympathetic nervous system is what we could consider our "action system"—it engages when our physiology needs to be engaged. It can be triggered by something as innocuous as a lively and active conversation or—in the throes of deep challenge, stress, and uncertainty—can also lead to a more threatening amygdala hijack. During an amygdala hijack, a physiological process whereby our amygdala triggers what is known as the "fight-or-flight response," our conscious mind shuts down (or at least takes a back seat) and our unconscious mind takes over. We are, in essence, acting without thinking.

"This is exactly what you don't want to happen," Rich explains. "In an uncertain environment, before you do anything, you need to first identify *what this is*. Only once you know what you're dealing with can you start to ask and answer, 'What do I now need to do?' For all of this to happen, you have to be able to engage in conscious thought."

However, deprogramming hundreds of thousands of years of evolution is easier said than done. This is why the SEALs' assessment and selection is so notoriously rigorous, and why it is built around what Rich, author of *The Attributes: 25 Hidden Drivers of Optimal Performance*, labels "attributes" rather than skills.

"We'd spend hundreds of hours jogging on beaches with boats on our heads or running while carrying huge telephone poles," Rich reminisces. "In all of my missions, every single one, do you know how many times I have carried a boat on my head? How many times I carried a telephone pole? Zero. The training wasn't about those skills—it was about identifying who had certain attributes, like those associated with grit, necessary to succeed in the kinds of environments we would face as a SEAL."

But although the SEALs' rigorous assessment and selection processes have been consistently capable of identifying the crème de la crème, Rich believed that with proper education and preparation the SEALs' optimal performance could be even better. Thus the "Mind Gym" was created.

"We wanted to ensure that when guys got to the point where the natural response would be a highjack of the sympathetic nervous system, they were instead able to engage their parasympathetic nervous system and exercise conscious thought and decision making. The Mind Gym was designed to help guys better understand the relationship between their mind and their physical response. We wanted them to have a working relationship with their entire nervous system."

Rich found that the best way, and indeed the only way, to engage the conscious mind in these environments of high uncertainty and high stress was to narrow that field of uncertainty to its smallest possible scope. Anything that could be made certain would further reduce that uncertainty field.

"As humans, it's a myth that we can multitask," explains Rich. "The truth is that we actually task switch. Every time we switch, though, that adds to our cognitive burden and means we have less mental capacity to deploy. When you're in these kinds of situations and environments, you don't have any mental capacity to spare."

But there are also instances, Rich explains, when we *can* seemingly multitask. This happens when one of the tasks we are doing does not require conscious thought but can instead be performed through what is colloquially called "muscle memory." The more and better we can hone the skills we will need to deploy in different situations, the more we can rely on our subconscious muscle memory to utilize those skills, and the more mental capacity we will free up to assess what the situation actually is and what we consciously need to do as a result.

"For SEALs," Rich says, "the three core skills are: shoot, move, and communicate. Practicing these to perfection and writing them to subconscious muscle memory frees up the conscious mind to assess and work through the uncertainties being faced.

"For shooting, it's about really understanding every single one of your weapons systems, about practicing transition drills to drop one and go to the other should anything jam or go wrong. For movement, this is basic. It could be driving; it could be walking or jogging. Basically it's the ability to move in a way that both enhances strategic position and can be telegraphed to team members. This gets us to communication—which comes in many flavors. There's a lot of nonverbal communication between guys in the field. There's the obvious verbal communication—boiled down to its most atomic level—where a single word and how it's communicated could mean an entire paragraph of things. There's knowing your radio system like the back of your hand so without thinking you can switch the dials just how you need to in order to call your air assets or whatever may be required.

"These are skills we would train on, then we would practice, then we would train on and practice again, and we would keep doing that until it was second nature. Then we would start throwing in uncertainty."

As Gary Brantley said of Mayor Keisha Lance Bottoms, we don't rise to the occasion in big moments; rather, we fall back on our training. This reality is exactly what Rich prepared his group of SEALs to be able to do with confidence and success.

"You have to have the skills down first," explains Rich. "Otherwise, you are under too much stress to be able to develop and master them in uncertain environments. But once you have those skills, we need to start testing them, straining them, stretching them in more and more uncertain ways."

But the benefit and, depending on your line of work, the necessity of preparing for the worst ahead of time is not limited to life-or-death military situations.

"We have a saying: 'If you're going to be stupid, you better be hard.' What it means," Rich shares, "is that if you aren't going to do the work to prepare, things are going to be harder for you. I tell my kids this all the time."

Thus, whether you are running a nighttime extraction mission, completing a project for your fourth-grade class, or delivering a big presentation, the key is to prepare beforehand. It's during the calm before any storm is even on the horizon that you want to anticipate and prepare for what could conceivably go wrong. This goes back to understanding our mental boundaries and what you can wholly control versus what you can't. The idea isn't to fixate on all the things outside your control that can possibly go wrong. Rather, the purpose is to identify and better understand those possibilities beforehand so that you can do the necessary planning and work ahead of time on the things that *are* within your control to make such events less likely, or at least make their negative impact less damaging.

You can't rid your life of all uncertainty, but you can reduce it. You can identify and prepare for what can go wrong and thus reduce your zone of uncertainty, as Gary and the city of Atlanta did. You can also prepare by being ready and able to respond and adapt when truly unforeseeable uncertainty arises, like Rich and the Navy SEALs do. If you're doing it right, you do both.

To go back to the presentation example, there are a multitude of actions you can take to prepare for this kind of event: You can master the skills involved in knowing exactly what you want to say and exactly what message you want others to take away. You can practice the presentation over and over until you can do it in your sleep, until you can seamlessly and confidently pick it up from any point should you be interrupted. You can familiarize yourself with the technological systems, and even bring backups, so that you are comfortable with them when the big moment comes. And you can prepare yourself to the point of knowing that you can give the presentation without even relying on the slides you may have developed, in case there is a technical malfunction—a situation

I personally experienced when I was presenting to more than a thousand people at the College Football Hall of Fame and the system that I had tested the day before malfunctioned.

Mastering the skills you'll need, and knowing you have mastered them, will not rid your life of uncertainties, but it can help inoculate you from uncertainty's worst effects. Preparation will better position you to succeed if and when the unforeseen and the unforeseeable come about. Waiting until you are put to the test, hoping upon hope that you will magically rise to the occasion, is a recipe for disaster. The answer lies in putting in the work beforehand, before things are bad. As Seneca wrote, "It is when times are good that you should gird yourself for tougher times ahead, for when Fortune is kind the soul can build defenses against her ravages." It's time to start building those defenses.

OWN Your Preparation

The Stoics found that the best way to build these necessary defenses to protect ownership of your mind was to identify what sorts of defenses you might need ahead of time. They did this through a practice they called *futurorum malorum præmeditatio*, or for those not fluent in dead languages, "negative visualization." The idea is to meditate upon and to actually start to visualize the worst-case scenario or scenarios. Once you have identified these, you are better positioned to understand them, pursue countermeasures to prevent them, and lessen their impact if they occur.

To make this concept more tangible and actionable, it can make sense to work through the three steps of the **OWN framework**:

OWN: Objective, Wrong, Nail

To do this, you begin by defining the **Objective** you're pursuing. Is it signing that big client? Is it getting an A on that important class project?

Is it completing a high-risk mission and getting everyone home safely? Be as clear as possible about the end result you seek, and specify what it looks like.

Once you have your Objective clearly identified, the second step is to put on your best pessimist's cap and think through all the things that can go **Wrong** in your pursuit of this Objective. Some of these things you will be able to prevent through your preparation—do what you can now to make sure they don't happen. Others you will only be able to minimize—do what you can to reduce the likelihood these will arise.

The third and final step in preparing for a worst-case scenario is to **Nail** the skills you will need in pursuing the Objective so that when the unforeseen and unforeseeable inevitably arise you will be able, as Rich explained, to fall back on your skills training and maximize the amount of your conscious mind you can allocate to identifying "what this is" and then "what you now need to do about it." OWN your preparation, and you are that much more likely to own the result you seek.

CHAPTER 4 TAKEAWAYS
. . . .

1. The more and the better you prepare, the less uncertainty you will face.
2. Despite even the best preparation, unforeseen and unforeseeable events and circumstances can and will arise.
3. **OWN** your preparation by taking these steps:
    a. Define your **Objective**.
    b. Think through everything that can go **Wrong** in the pursuit of that Objective, and do what you can ahead of time to prevent them or at least minimize their likelihood of occurring.
    c. **Nail** the skills you will need as you pursue your Objective.

OWN Worksheet

OBJECTIVE:

What can go Wrong:	How you can minimize this or prevent it from happening:
1.	a.
	b.
	c.
	d.
2.	a.
	b.
	c.
	d.
3.	a.
	b.
	c.
	d.

Skills to Nail ahead of time:

I.	III.
II.	IV.

CHAPTER 5

· · · · · · · · · · · · · · · · · · · ·

A Crisis Is a Terrible Thing to Waste (*Every Catastrophe Creates Opportunity*)

When preparation fails to prevent
the worst from occurring, you can
turn the worst to your advantage.

We could see the wave coming a month or so before it hit. Our clients in Asia had already had to "pause" their accounts with us. Travel was completely banned, so what help did they need with pricing and revenue management for vacation rentals? Our African clients had started doing the same, and in Europe it seemed only a matter of days.

With 90 percent of our revenue coming from within the United States, we had been largely insulated, health-wise and economically, up to this point from the pandemic that was making its way across the globe. However, we knew that past performance was not an accurate indicator of future success. For all the talk of American exceptionalism, the truth was that the virus did not care about national borders. It was coming for our clients, and thus it was coming for us.

As you might have guessed, this all played out during February 2020. It is probably difficult to get back into the state of mind you may have had at the time, but chances are you thought of COVID-19 as something that happened on the other side of the world. While for the sake of my country, my clients, and the health and well-being of my friends, family, and loved ones, I hoped this was true, I also had to come to terms with the likelihood that in relatively short order we would all find ourselves in the same position as so many others before us.

As international markets closed to inbound travelers, and as some airports closed entirely, effectively killing any sort of travel whatsoever for our island-based clients, reality appeared to be about ten times worse than my preconceived worst-case scenario. Just a month prior, in an act completely unrelated to the global pandemic, we had sublet our physical office and made the entire company remote. That is why I was now huddled in a WeWork call room, conducting our weekly executive team meeting virtually rather than working things out with my colleagues in person.

"Assuming revenue goes to zero, how many months can we stay alive?" I asked our CFO, Karen.

"At our current spend? Not even six," she responded.

Ouch. Less than half a year, with no indication of when, or if, any light at the end of the COVID tunnel would come.

"Obviously we can stretch that out," she continued. "There are some costs we can at least defer temporarily, and anything we can possibly do to hold on to some revenue will be crucial."

Still, I had to ask the question I imagined we were all thinking about.

"Would doing all of that just slow down our approach to the cliff's edge?" I asked. "Say we make it eight or even ten months instead of six. If there is no travel, if we have no clients, the end result is the same. We're just taking longer to get there."

I watched my computer screen as my team let this sink in over video, their faces drawn. We had all been so caught up in buying time that we had not thought about what that extra time would—or would not—get us.

"Unless in that extra time we buy we are able to build a bridge over the cliff's edge," Cliff said (yes, that's his real name).

We all just looked at him on the screen, waiting for him to go on.

"What I mean is that right now no one really knows how long this will go on. It could be three months, or it could be three years."

We nodded in agreement. This wasn't exactly comforting.

"But," he continued, "if each day we can buy two more through cost cutting and increased revenue, we can at least stay alive long enough to give ourselves a chance to make it to the other side."

"That sounds great," I responded. "The only issue is that revenue is going down right now. How can we grow it if clients are pausing and canceling?"

As that reality sunk in, it was as if the oxygen had left our virtual conference room. And then it hit me.

"Unless," I said, everyone looking at me in anticipation, "we can go forward by first going backward."

Their confusion and disappointment were clear. What the hell was I talking about?

"Think about it: if our clients don't survive, it doesn't matter how many days we 'buy'; we won't have a viable business on the other side of this."

Again, my realistic pessimism was not exactly inspiring my team.

"The number-one thing we can do right now is help our clients stay in business," I said.

"Sure," Karen chimed in. "But how can we do that?"

"By doing more for them," I said, "and making it cheaper."

I watched as the idea washed over my team members one at a time. It resonated. Now it was time to get to work.

Two days later, we reached out to every single client we had.

"Until June, every single bill you have from us will be cut in half," we told them. "We know things are tough right now and are likely to get even more difficult in the coming weeks and months. That is why we want to make it easier, cheaper, and indeed possible for you to keep us around for when things pick up, because at that time you will need us more than ever. We want to be there for you."

You're probably wondering how in the world we thought we could extend the life of the company by, in the best case, cutting in half the money coming in. The answer was that, at the same time, we were quietly cutting our outgoing spend by the same amount. In an incredibly brave and selfless move, every single member of the executive team took a tremendous pay cut in order to cover the loss in revenue the price cuts created.

But we didn't stop there. We knew our clients could not just wait for travel to magically restart if they were to stay in business. They needed to do something different, and they needed to do it fast. This is why, at the same time we announced our price cuts, we also launched a number of new services to support our clients. From our "Emergency Planning in a Box," in which our executive team would conduct a deep dive with our clients on their finances to help them chart their own path through the storm; to our staffing support to help people in our industry who had been furloughed or laid off because of the crisis; to even the assistance we offered to clients so they could repurpose their homes as housing for first responders rather than vacation rentals, we looked at the skill sets we possessed internally, as well as the immediate needs of our clients, and began to offer help in any and every way we thought we might be able to add value.

And it paid off. The truth was that at the time the move was a bet. We had no idea if travel would restart by June. It was quite possible we would get to June and find that travel was down so much that clients could not keep us even at 50 percent of our normal price, much less our full price. But it was a risk we were willing to take, and one we believed we had to take. If travel did not pick up by the summer, it was unlikely most companies in our industry would survive at all. However, if they did, we wanted to be well positioned to deliver on our promise to our clients.

And so, the week before Memorial Day, when Florida's governor began again allowing vacation rentals, we were there for our clients, making sure they could handle the flood of new bookings and make the most of them.

As the year progressed, more and more of our clients expanded with us instead of canceling, and more and more sent us notes about how the year they thought would kill their business was now a record year—and they attributed that performance to the work we'd done for them. As one even told me personally, "A lot of vendors reached out to say, 'We are all in this together,' but you were the only one who actually showed it with actions." In this way, we were able to view the crisis through a new lens. It has been difficult. There have been times when it felt like hell. But so far, the challenges we faced ended up making us stronger as a team and stronger as a company. The crisis made us better.

Polishing the Stone

Long before humans even knew what a virus was, the Stoic philosopher Epictetus said:

> Every difficulty in life presents us with an opportunity to turn inward and to invoke our own submerged inner resources. The trials we endure can and should introduce us to our strengths . . . Dig deeply. You possess strengths you might not realize you have. Find the right one. Use it.

Epictetus knew that preparation can take us only so far. No matter how much and how hard we work at preparing, certain difficulties, and indeed crises, will still arise. Epictetus also knew, though, that it is when things are the hardest that we are the most stretched and thus learn what we are really capable of. Rather than suggesting that we lament our bad luck, the Stoics advise that we instead view crises as opportunities for growth and improvement. In fact, in certain instances, crises can create the very definition of who we are and how we will be remembered. Think of leaders like Franklin Delano Roosevelt during the Great Depression, Winston Churchill during World War II, and Abraham Lincoln during the Civil War (he reportedly had Marcus Aurelius's *Meditations* on his nightstand at the time he was assassinated).[21] It was by facing and taking on the unimaginable crises of their respective times that these men grew as leaders. Pushing themselves to the very limits, they refused to be deterred by personal or professional setbacks, and in so doing they elevated the concept of mind ownership to an entirely new level. Through the worst moments of their times, they demonstrated what they were capable of, both to themselves and to the world around and after them.

As Epictetus also said, "What would have become of Hercules, do you think, if there had been no lion, hydra, stag or boar—and no savage criminals to rid the world of? What would he have done in the absence of such challenges?" Greatness is defined by the obstacles it overcomes, and thus we should embrace these obstacles. "Pressure," says Saint Augustine, "is inescapable." And while there are those who "grumble under these pressures and complain," Saint Augustine goes on, there are also people who "under the same pressure [do] not complain, for it is the friction which polishes [them]." When faced with our own pressures, we each have the opportunity to choose to let that pressure own our mind and as a result grind us down to something less than what we started with, or to own our mind and use that friction to our advantage by polishing ourselves to make us something more and better than we were before.

Loc-ME, Loc-U, Locus

How we react to a crisis or other outside event is often a by-product of how we view events in our life more generally. Are events happening *to* us such that we are mere passive bystanders, or are we able to control, or at least influence, the outcomes? In psychology, this concept is known as "locus of control." As Professor Philip Zimbardo writes, "A locus of control orientation is a belief about whether the outcomes of our actions are contingent on what we do (internal control orientation) or on events outside our personal control (external control orientation)."[22]

Whether we have an internal or external locus of control has far-reaching effects on our life and our happiness throughout it. A study that followed thousands of children from birth found that children who at an early age showed an internal locus of control "were less likely to be overweight at age 30 . . . [and] less likely to describe their health as poor, or show high levels of psychological stress."[23] The explanation given by the researcher was that "children with a more internal locus of control behave more healthily as adults because they have greater confidence in their ability to influence outcomes through their own actions." She also noted that these children "may also have higher self-esteem." The more control you believe you exert over your life, the better you feel about that life and thus about yourself.

Enter the Dragon

If you're looking for someone with an enviably strong internal control orientation, Bruce Lee is hard to beat. From his health, to his career, to his mental development, Bruce Lee knew *he* was in the driver's seat and the hero of his own story. In the 1960s, an age of rampant racism in Hollywood and elsewhere, Lee knew that if he gave authorship of the story that was his life to anyone else, he would be relegated to sidekick at best. He also knew he was far better than that.

This strong sense of internal control was put to the test right as Bruce Lee was poised to get his big break, his daughter, Shannon, writes in *Be Water, My Friend: The True Teachings of Bruce Lee*. In 1968, during one of his rigorous home workouts, Bruce Lee injured his back to such an extent that "the doctor told him he would have to prepare for the idea that he would never do martial arts again, that he may in fact never walk again without considerable pain."[24] Someone with an external locus of control, indeed someone with a less well-formed *internal* locus of control, might have given up right then. How could he do five hundred one-handed push-ups to start his day if he could not even walk without pain?

But remember, this was Bruce Lee. This was the man who believed it was not the obstacle that mattered, but rather your response to it. He wrote:

> It is not a shame to be knocked down. The important thing is to ask when you're being knocked down, "why am I being knocked down?" If a person can reflect in this way, then there is hope for this person. Defeat is a state of mind; no one is ever defeated until defeat has been accepted as a reality. To me, defeat in anything is merely temporary, and its punishment is but an urge for me to exert greater effort to achieve my goal. Defeat simply tells me that something is wrong in my doing; it is a path leading to success and truth.[25]

Bruce Lee decided that defeat was not something that happened *to* him. Only he could allow himself to be defeated, and he would *not* be defeated.

Reflecting back on his injury, Bruce Lee saw it with more than a little silver lining:

> Sure my back screwed me up good for a year but with every adversity comes a blessing because a shock acts as a reminder to oneself that we must not get stale in routine. With adversity you are shocked to higher levels if you allow yourself to go beyond your current circumstances.[26]

The injury did not set him back; rather, it helped him propel himself forward. His internal locus of control enabled Bruce Lee to turn events on their head. Something that an average person would have used as an excuse to give up, Bruce Lee made into good fortune. That is why he would never be accused of being "average." He took advantage of every crisis as an opportunity.

The Impossible First

It was 2008, and Colin O'Brady was having a hard time looking beyond his current circumstances.[27] His dream trip around the world, one for which he had worked every summer during college to save up for, had in a few seconds turned into a complete nightmare. One moment he was sipping beers in a beachside bar in Koh Tao off of mainland Thailand, the next he was writhing in pain on the sand, a kerosene-soaked jump rope wrapped around his body. What had seemed like innocent fun turned into a near-deadly mistake when Colin mistimed his jump and tripped over the rope.

Now, after Colin had sought more specialized medical care on the mainland to treat his injury, his mother, who had traveled around the world to be at his side, was asking him, "What do you want to do when you get out of here? Let's set a goal." This was days after the Thai doctor told Colin he would never walk normally again, and Colin could not see the point.[28]

"Mom, are you kidding me?" Colin asked back. "My life is over."

But Colin's mother was not having it. Crisis has a way of not just showing us what *we* are capable of, but showing us what those around us are capable of as well.

"Do me a favor, close your eyes," she responded. "I want you to set a goal [for] after you get out of here, Colin. Visualize it. Picture yourself doing it. Grab onto it."

Perhaps to humor his mother, perhaps to express his gratitude to her for putting her life on hold to come to his bedside on the other side of the world, Colin did as she asked.

"In that moment," he writes in his powerful memoir *The Impossible First*, "for whatever reason, I saw myself completing a triathlon. Something I had never done before." Colin's mom did not look down at his legs and ask him to set a more realistic goal. No, instead she kept her gaze fixed on his eyes and responded, "I can already see you crossing the finish line."

In Chicago, eighteen months after his accident, Colin did just that, completing the Chicago Triathlon. Except Colin did not just complete it—he won it. The next Monday, Colin quit his job in finance and began a life he would have never imagined, or perhaps even attempted, had it not been for his accident and that nudge from his mother.

First, he became a professional triathlete and member of the US National Team, for which he raced in twenty-five countries and on six continents.

Later, he became an adventurer and world-record holder, simultaneously setting the world records for the Explorers Grand Slam and the Seven Summits. In the first event, Colin summited the tallest peak on every continent, including Mount Everest, and skied the last degree to the North and South Poles. As if that wasn't impressive enough, Colin completed this feat at such a blisteringly fast pace that he set the world record for the Seven Summits, the peaks without the poles, at the same time.

And still later, he became a "world firster," tackling and achieving feats that no human had ever accomplished before, such as, in 2018, the world's first solo, unsupported, and completely human-powered crossing of Antarctica.

"The best way to deal with a crisis," a mentor once told Colin, "is not to have it in the first place."[29] In other words, try to avoid crises by preparing ahead of time as Rich and Gary demonstrated in chapter four. But since even the best preparation cannot prevent every possible crisis, the question then becomes, how do you respond when a crisis inevitably occurs?

Upon reflection, Colin sees his own crisis as a sort of domino. "When one domino falls, everything changes down the line and the best we can do is be ready with a new plan, a new adaptation," he writes.[30]

Indeed, one night, years after the accident, lying alone in his tent during the Antarctic crossing, Colin looked down at his beaten body and came to a realization. "Our defeats can't be separated from our victories. Scars and triumphs both make us who we are . . . The good and the bad couldn't be separated. What I was, and how I'd come to be there, tucked into my little world on the ice, was a consequence of every event in my life."[31]

Colin now reflects, "We're all occasionally weighed down by our burdens . . . My burden, it seemed, was also my salvation."[32]

And the Plural of *Crisis* Is . . .

Colin O'Brady's isn't the only inspiring story of an athlete overcoming incredible odds. What should have been the final step of a lifelong pursuit quickly turned into an abrupt halt for Christopher George. For as long as he could remember, Christopher had wanted to represent his country, Trinidad and Tobago, in the Olympics. As the captain of the nation's water polo team, Christopher thought he was at the cusp of doing just this when, in 2011, he led the team to its first ever qualification for the Pan American Games, the Olympic qualifier for his region. Christopher was ecstatic. That is, he *was* ecstatic until the Amateur Swimming Association of Trinidad and Tobago, the governing body, decided not to send the team, having preemptively decided that the team would not be competitive enough to justify the trip.

This decision led Christopher to walk away from water polo, the sport that he loved and knew he excelled in, but he was not yet ready to give up on his dream of representing his country in the Olympics. Concerned that a path to the Olympics would be unlikely in a team sport, Christopher rededicated himself and decided to pursue judo, a sport he had recently become fascinated by. Just a year later, he was Trinidad's national judo champion. And so began his new journey in continued pursuit of his Olympic dream.

In the intervening years, life went on. Christopher attended Georgia Tech, earning a degree in engineering. From there he took a job with BP, and his employer transferred him across the ocean to Aberdeen, Scotland. And at every step, Christopher kept his Olympic dream alive, as well as his judo training.

Upon his arrival in Aberdeen, Christopher joined a local judo club and made a list of every single tournament in Scotland and northern England he could compete in to continue to hone his skills. He continued to improve, competing in the Commonwealth Games in Glasgow, Scotland, in 2014 and even winning a bronze medal at the Central American Championship the same year.

Later that year, however, his journey seemed again to be at a cross-roads. With oil prices plummeting, BP decided to bring all its expatriates back to their home countries. BP was going through a restructuring and offered voluntary separation packages to those who wanted to leave. Christopher had a decision to make: try to weather the storm in a forlorn company or double down on his Olympic journey. Christopher chose the pursuit of his Olympian ambitions. With the money he received from the severance package, he decided it was time to go all in on his pursuit of the Olympics.

Shortly after making this decision, Christopher followed the advice of a fellow judo competitor and started training at a club in Schenectady, New York, led by Jason Morris, an elite judo instructor, and four-time Olympian and Olympic silver medalist. Christopher trained at the club six days a week and competed every other week in a tournament in the tristate area.

"In a few months I got forty to fifty matches under my belt," he says. "It wasn't international competition, but it was still like sandpaper smoothing the rough edges of my ashlar."

But while Christopher's Olympic plans seemed to be on track, it wasn't long before they went off the rails again. In February 2016, Christopher was at a training camp in Paris and also at the end of his tether. Coming off the high of his successes in 2015, Christopher was now laid low. He had been knocked out in the first round in his last tournament, was getting pummeled daily by ten past Olympic and world champions with whom he was training in the camp, and was now completely out of the money he had allocated to get him to the Olympics in Rio de Janeiro that year. Ready to quit while mere steps away from his goal, Christopher called Amanda Johnson, his sports psychologist.

Amanda heard Christopher out and commiserated with him about the crisis that seemed to be building. And then she told Christopher to let it go. Let go of the expectations, let go of where he thought he should be, and let go of any thoughts of what would happen in the next three months and the Olympic Games. She told him the important thing *right now* was to "take a deep breath, take one step, and go to training."

Christopher heeded her advice. Finishing the training camp, he once again rededicated himself to his pursuit. His father helped him with the money to get back to London. A MakeAChamp crowdfunding campaign elicited donations from 143 individual donors. Then Judo Trinidad and Tobago stepped in to sponsor Christopher to the Pan American Senior Championships in Cuba. All of this support and funding added up and helped nudge him along in his journey.

"At first I thought, *You have to do this on your own!*" Christopher admits. "But it really is like that quote from Marcus Aurelius: 'Don't be ashamed to need help. Like a soldier storming a wall, you have a mission to accomplish. And if you've been wounded and you need a comrade to pull you up? So what?' Yes, I needed help, and I was thankful to receive it."

At the Pan American Senior Championships in Cuba, the final tournament before the Olympic cycle, Christopher finished in the top seven competitors, securing his place as one of the top five athletes in the region and earning him a continental bid for the Olympic Games. In so doing, Christopher became the first person ever from Trinidad and Tobago, and the entire English-speaking Caribbean, to qualify for the Olympics through an official bid.

And so, in August 2016, Christopher George achieved his lifetime ambition of becoming an Olympian, marching out and representing Trinidad and Tobago at the Rio Olympics. But this was not the end of his journey or his learning. The accelerated training and competition schedule required for Christopher to switch sports entirely and become an Olympian in a few short years had taken a toll on his body. In 2017, his Olympic dream fulfilled, Christopher had to have a double hip replacement. And yet again, Christopher did not let this crisis negatively define him or his potential.

Speaking to me about it now, Christopher explains his mindset. "After the surgery," he says, "I wanted to prove to myself that athletics were not over for me, and so I went back to train [again] for water polo."

In 2018, Christopher again qualified for Trinidad and Tobago's water polo national team and was named its captain. Looking back to what drove him, Christopher quotes Epictetus: "Lameness is an impediment to the leg, but not to the will."

Christopher's life and dreams have now moved on yet again—he is now an attorney with his own thriving practice.

"The truth is," Christopher shares, "the same challenges continue [for me] today [as they did throughout my athletic career]. Clients come in with their problems; I have invoices that some people don't pay; I never know what's around the corner. Everything I have been through, though, has taught me that I can and will get through it. It comes down to me just focusing on what is right in front of me and to getting done what I can do today." After all, a crisis is what you make of it. As Christopher has learned time and again, by preparing and focusing on what you can control, you can make the most of every situation, defining for yourself how you will respond rather than letting the crisis define you.

Providing a Lifeline

Regardless of who you are or how "blessed" your life has been to date, you have no doubt had to deal with your own fair share of crises. Whether they are the "daily tragedies" of traffic jams that make you miss crucial appointments, or events that are far more serious, there have been bumps along the way in your journey to where you are now.

And yet, as surely as you are reading this now, you are here, in this moment. Not only are you here, but you are also a product of *all* that came before to bring you here. Maybe you have not had your lifelong dream stomped on by a faceless bureaucracy, and more than likely you have not suffered a terrible physical injury and been told you will never walk again normally, but just as Christopher and Colin managed to use their own low points as launching pads for their future high points, perhaps you have done the same, without realizing it.

Understanding this, acknowledging it, appreciating it, and identifying *how* you did it, and perhaps how you could have done it even more effectively, is the key to not wasting your own present and future crises. How can you start? By taking the advice of Epictetus's own teacher, Gaius Musonius Rufus, who said, "Do not be irked by difficult circumstances, but reflect on how many things have already happened to you in life in ways that you did not wish, and yet they have turned out for the best."[33] A practical way to do just this is to go through a process known as the "lifeline exercise" in order to see how, in many cases, the low moments in your life actually helped lead to your high moments. Here's how you'll use the worksheet at the end of this chapter to create your own lifeline exercise (the x-axis of this chart represents your age, and the y-axis represents your relative level of fulfillment and satisfaction):

1. Start by thinking of ten events in your life, the five highest highs and the five lowest lows, and plot these points at the corresponding age and level of satisfaction or fulfillment they brought you. For example, if a high point was at age fifteen, then you should have a point marking that event well above the dashed line at the

fifteen-year position on your graph. The same goes for low-point events. Draw a line connecting all of these points as a single thread through your life thus far.

2. Now, taking each low-point event in turn, rather than focusing on all the bad that came out of it, think about what from that event eventually led to one or more of the future highs. This is not to say that bad did not also come from the event; it's just that those bad effects are not the focus of this exercise. Focus instead on which doors closed, or windows opened, and set you on a path to reach that later high or highs.

3. If your last point is on a low, revisit how a past low led to a future high, and start brainstorming ways you might be able to turn this current low into a future high. The same goes for a low you will no doubt face after having completed this exercise.

4. Revisit and repeat this exercise as often as you find appropriate and useful.

CHAPTER 5 TAKEAWAYS

1. Every human being suffers hardship and numerous crises throughout life.

2. Rather than lament or bemoan this fact of life, you have the opportunity to develop a strong internal locus of control. By doing this, you can turn each crisis into an opportunity and in the process make yourself better and stronger.

3. To identify your own past strength through crisis and help prepare you for future crises, go through the lifeline exercise to see how past low points have actually made your later high points possible.

Lifeline Exercise

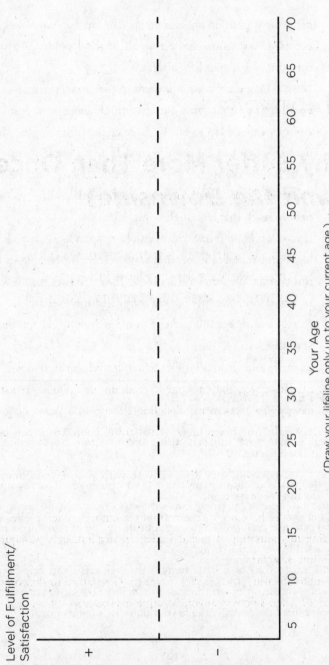

Level of Fulfillment/ Satisfaction

Your Age
(Draw your lifeline only up to your current age.)

CHAPTER 6

. . . .

Why Suffer More Than Once? (*Limit the Downside*)

> Despite your best efforts, there will be
> unavoidable suffering along the way,
> but you can absolutely limit its effects.

Trademark the entire exec team is losing their collective shit right now."

That was the message I read on my phone backstage, having just pitched my fledgling startup to a panel of judges at PhoCusWright, the preeminent global travel conference then being hosted in Los Angeles.

"Everyone is saying they'll never work with you or your company again," the next message read.

What should have been a moment of triumph, or at least relief after presenting to thousands of global leaders in my industry, was quickly turning into a nightmare.

"And by the way," the next text came in, "I've talked to the competition judges. There's no way anyone's voting for you now."

The texts all came from the head of corporate development at the largest public company in my industry at the time. For years we had been in talks about different ways we could work together, and they were consistently collegial. We had even signed a partnership agreement in the past and, as far as I knew, had a friendly working relationship. Now all of that seemed to have disappeared over the course of just a few minutes without me even realizing it.

What had set them off? Why was everyone "losing their collective shit" and vowing never to work with me? It came back to a question one of the pitch competition judges asked as I wrapped up my presentation. Or rather, if I'm being honest, it came back to *my answer* to the question the judge asked.

My company was an entirely new kind of marketplace for vacation rentals. Rather than connecting travelers with homes to book for a night or a week at a time, it connected owners of the homes with professional companies that could manage all the work on their behalf over the course of an entire year. No one had ever successfully built anything like it, and though it was early days, my new startup was doubling in transaction volume and revenue every single month.

The panelist asked a question many must have had on their minds. "Why wouldn't X [the large public company in this industry] just do this itself, effectively killing your business?"

I didn't intend my response to be derogatory, inflammatory, or even controversial. I thought I was sharing what everyone else already knew when I said, "But X doesn't build new products. Its entire strategy is to buy up existing businesses and roll them together. In fact, it has already purchased thirty-five companies following this exact approach."

However, the fact that everything I said was correct and could be confirmed in the company's own records did nothing to assuage the fury of the executive team at the company in question.

I wasn't sure how to respond to the flurry of text messages bombarding my phone. I wasn't sure if I *should* respond. Looking for consolation, I went to a friend of mine who also happened to be a startup founder attending the conference and told him what had just happened.

"Dude!" he said. "There goes your exit strategy. You better make that right!"

Not the comfort I was looking for. Thinking that perhaps some fresh air would help clear my head, I left the conference hall and made my way to the hotel lobby. Before I could safely make it out the door, the chief product officer of the large company in question buttonholed me against the wall. In front of numerous luminaries in the travel industry, not to mention his own company's head of public relations, the executive proceeded to unleash a torrent of f-bombs, the likes of which I had never before received.

As one final parting shot before he allowed me to escape, the executive closed with this: "Great idea, though. I look forward to stealing it."

The Oxford Comma

This was hardly the coming-out party I had pictured for myself and my company when I was accepted into the prestigious pitch competition.

Trying to prevent an emotional tailspin, I finally got outside, put on my headphones, and with some Vampire Weekend blasting, took a walk around downtown Los Angeles. As much as I wanted to enjoy the fact that it was November and seventy degrees and sunny, that I had just run the gauntlet of presenting on stage at the biggest conference in my entire industry, and that my company was doing quite well and attracting interest from a number of investors, I kept finding myself thinking back to the company I had offended. About what it would mean for our ability to ever work together. About what would happen if the company decided to follow through on its threat of "stealing" my idea.

But every time my mind unhelpfully jumped to these thoughts, I also thought back to Seneca's words of wisdom: "We suffer more often in imagination than in reality." Looking around, knowing what was actually true and real in that moment, and the position I and my company were in, what suffering was there in reality? Or was it all in my mind?

Newly clearheaded and confident, I stepped back into the conference hotel. Within minutes of stepping into the lobby, the cofounder and COO of the company in question came up to me.

"What the hell did you do?" he asked me with a laugh. "I missed your presentation, and when I walked into the hotel everybody kept saying, 'Fuck that Andrew McConnell.'"

I uncomfortably smiled back at his apparent glee.

"I asked what you did," he went on. "They said, 'He went on stage and said we didn't build new products—we just bought companies.'"

I watched him, wondering what would come next.

"I said, 'Yeah, that's exactly what we do. That's our entire strategy. That was the business plan I wrote up when I started the company. What's the big deal?'"

My body immediately released the tension it had been carrying, and I sighed audibly without meaning to.

"That's what I thought!" I burst out.

We had a laugh together and then parted ways.

Later that night, I was back onstage in the conference hall. This time I was shaking hands with the conference presenters and receiving the award from the judges who had just named my company the "Most Innovative Startup in Travel" globally.

From the time I first walked offstage and looked at my phone, I had every reason to suffer in my imagination. Every person I spoke to, every signal I received, told me I had just created a disaster for my company and myself. And yet, as is so often the case, all the horrors I could and did run through my mind failed to come to pass. All they did was make it more difficult for me to enjoy the moment that was.

Fortunately, the suffering in my imagination was cut short when a more positive reality quickly occurred, but as I'm sure you've experienced yourself, this isn't always—or even often—the case.

Whether it is dreading an imagined event well before it happens (or an event that never happens) or relentlessly replaying something negative that we heard, felt, or experienced in the past, far too often we find ourselves suffering more than once: We suffer before the event by worrying about it. We suffer during the event (if indeed the event ever occurs). And when we allow the event to play on a loop in our mind, we continue to suffer unnecessarily long after the event.

Why? What good comes from this? The best case is that the imagined event we're dreading never comes to pass. In that case, we have technically suffered only once, in our preimagining of it. Even then, depending on the circumstances, this replaying can last for days or even years. And we didn't need to suffer in the first place. The problem existed only in our mind. All of this worrying is distinguishable from imagining and preparing for worst-case scenarios, as we discussed in chapter four. If in imagining worst-case scenarios, you are then doing the necessary work to prevent those scenarios from occurring or mitigating their negative impact, this is time well spent. If you are instead just playing what is effectively a horror movie on loop in your mind, this is purely detrimental.

What about in those cases where there was actual suffering? In such instances, ask yourself the question Seneca posed: "What is the point of dragging up sufferings that are over, of being miserable now, because you were miserable then?" Wasn't it enough to be miserable at the time? Why prolong your suffering? Once is surely enough.

E-Sign on the Dotted Line

Any technology startup founder has experienced their fair share of challenges and opportunities for suffering along the way. But Tom Gonser, who founded and built DocuSign, perhaps experienced more than most, giving him every excuse in the book to pre- and post-suffer many crises along the way. However, as a serial entrepreneur, Tom never fell into this trap, nor did he allow his team to do so.

"In the sixteen years it took to go from an idea to a public company," Tom admits, "there was a lot of suffering along the way. But we never suffered the same thing more than once. There's no point."

This is coming from someone who had already successfully founded and scaled multiple businesses before DocuSign. Tom's prior experience certainly served him well as he launched what has since become the global standard for e-signature. But while his experience helped Tom avoid some suffering, he couldn't avoid it all. It started, perhaps inevitably, just as the company signed its first big contract.

"Like most startups," Tom explains, "we decided to start off by going after smaller companies first. Yes, the contract sizes were also smaller, but SMBs [small and medium-sized businesses] just don't have anywhere near the same sort of bureaucracies or long sales cycles that bigger companies do, and which can be a death trap for a fledgling startup."

This bottom-up approach helped DocuSign land early clients, but its small size was doing little to convince outside investors that this was a company capable of venture scale, that is, that it had the potential to provide more than ten times the return on their investment. That changed when Tom landed zipForm as a client. At that time, zipForm counted 60 percent of US real estate agents as users of its software. This meant that through its integration, DocuSign would suddenly be in the hands of one hundred thousand different users in a matter of months. This megadeal gave investors the validation they required to write a big check to the company, and in short order DocuSign closed its Series A round of investment.

And then . . . nothing happened. Yes, DocuSign was integrated with zipForm, and, yes, with a click of a button, real estate agents could now send contracts out virtually for e-signing, making the process that much simpler and faster, but, no, nobody was actually doing so. When given the option to click a button or print out the document and physically chase down wet signatures, the agents chose the analog option ten times out of ten.

The economics of DocuSign's deal with zipForm were based on usage, and without it, the megadeal was worthless to DocuSign. Clearly, DocuSign needed to do something differently.

"We thought we'd covered all our bases," says Tom, thinking back on it now. "Before we ever launched, we sat down with exactly these same types of people and businesses, and we had built the product around everything they said they needed."

What they had said they needed was not an e-signature solution—or rather more correctly, not *just* an e-signature solution.

"When we first came to them with the idea of e-signature, everyone said they would never use it," Tom explains.

Why wouldn't they use something that was so much simpler, easier, and faster and could make the logistics of their business more efficient?

"They were more worried about the entire workflow," Tom goes on. "The signature part of it was a piece, but just a piece. How would they know who really provided that signature? When they did so? How it was sent and received? And where would all of that data be tracked and stored, and how would it get into their existing systems? We quickly learned we weren't building an e-signature product after all; we were building an automated workflow platform, and e-signature was one component of that."

This made the lack of usage of DocuSign's product all the more surprising and confusing. DocuSign had done everything it needed to do to address these concerns! Still, rather than sit in his office and prolong the suffering, Tom did what a great founder does: he went into the field to sit with prospective clients and understand *why* they weren't using the product they had said they wanted.

"I'd sit with them and walk them through each step and how it integrated with what they already did, just faster and easier," says Tom. "Basically, everyone responded, 'This is a game changer! This is going to allow me to close so many more deals!'"

But Tom now knew not to stop asking questions there. When he then posed the follow-up question "So will you use it?" they all said no. Their reason? It was too new and unproven.

"What if an ID gets stolen?" they asked. "Is this even legal?" they wondered. Tom had a ready response for every question and concern. "What law can I tell you we adhere to? Can I explain the technology we use to keep your ID safe?" It wasn't enough. Being right was not the same thing as being believed.

"Look," they came back, "I'm not a lawyer or technologist. I have no way of knowing if what you're saying is true." Early adopters these were not.

At this point, having spent years trying to build a product that did exactly what these potential clients said they wanted and needed, only for them to say they wouldn't use it, Tom would have been forgiven for giving up. It would be understandable if Tom had allowed himself to be taken over by the suffering that led to this point, the suffering of the failed launch in this moment, and the future suffering of worrying that he'd never be able to get the company off the ground. But that's not what a mind owner would do, and that wasn't what Tom did, either. Brainstorming ways to earn DocuSign the validation these smaller clients apparently demanded, Tom asked, "What if Microsoft used it? Or what if the big banks used it? Would that give you confidence?" The unanimous affirmation was deafening.

Tom and DocuSign had suffered a setback, but they weren't going to suffer more than once. Going back to the drawing board, they flipped their entire sales strategy on its head. No longer could they afford to avoid the corporate bureaucracies of enterprise clients. They were going to have to navigate them head-on if they were going to get anywhere.

In addition, enterprise clients had their own sets of demands and requirements, from custom integrations to far more onerous security protocols. Slowly but surely DocuSign ticked each one off, and within a matter of months Microsoft signed on as a client. Not long after, Wells Fargo signed up as well, at the same time publishing an industry white paper telling other financial institutions that if they were going to use an e-signature platform, it should be DocuSign because it was the most secure. DocuSign was off to the races.

As you can probably surmise, the suffering didn't stop there, however. At one point, DocuSign was on the cusp of signing a contract with a major overnight company that was worth ten times DocuSign's *entire* revenue at that time when the deal blew up over the prospective customer's demand that DocuSign white-label the product under the customer's brand. At another point, Tom approached a popular software company, then worth $4 billion, about a partnership integration, only to have the software company turn him down and then turn around and buy a competitor in order to compete with DocuSign directly. At yet another point, a change in government regulations on student lending killed off nearly a quarter of DocuSign's business overnight, making it impossible for the company to raise the next round of financing it needed to continue to scale the business.

In each instance, the challenges DocuSign faced, and the pain it felt, were real. But in each instance, Tom made sure neither he nor his team suffered "more in imagination than reality," as Seneca advised. When DocuSign refused to accept the overnight company's terms for the massive deal, Tom and the team didn't let the suffering linger. They just went back to work, building DocuSign, and its brand and reputation, globally. Years later, the company in question came back and said it actually wanted and needed the DocuSign brand on its signature process because of the greater validation and credibility it provided. And rather than worry about the threat from the software company that had acquired a competing e-signature business, Tom remained confident in DocuSign's strategy of being a workflow management platform, not just an e-signature tool. As a result, DocuSign didn't just survive after that software company purchased the competitor—it thrived even more than before and is now a public company with a market capitalization of nearly $50 billion. And all those investors who were too scared to invest in DocuSign after the change in government regulations? DocuSign's Series A investor jumped in to fill the void, and in the process turned its $16 million investment in the company into nearly $700 million when DocuSign went public a few years later.

Now, as an investor himself, Tom does his best to share his painful lessons with other founders he advises and mentors.

"Challenges are an inevitable part of building a company," Tom admits. "Hell, they're an inevitable part of life. That being said, how and even if you choose to suffer, that's up to you."

"But," Tom concludes, "even when you do, there's never a good reason to suffer the same thing more than once. Suffering the same failure more than once is silly."

Re: Suffering

Suffering is going to be an inevitable part of your life. No matter how good you are at following Gary and Rich's examples of diligent preparation in chapter four, no matter how much you follow Christopher and Colin's examples from chapter five and turn a crisis into a boon, there will still be times of unavoidable suffering that arise. Things won't always go your way. You will at some point face your share of setbacks in the journey that is life. But there's no good reason to suffer now through your imagining of some potential future suffering, just as there's no benefit to suffering now while ruminating on some suffering from the past. One may never actually occur, the other did, but is now over.

Allowing that suffering to live in your mind—indeed, allowing it to own your mind any longer than the actual duration of the suffering—is to fall prey to Marcus Aurelius's observation: "How much more harmful are the consequences of anger and grief than the circumstances that aroused them in us!" In other words, the negative feelings we experience in obsessing over past or future suffering inevitably cause us even more harm than the instance of suffering itself. To prevent these more harmful consequences, you need to stop allowing the suffering to take over your mind. But how?

Working through the "suffering decision tree" below is a good place to start. Recognizing you cannot always turn off the suffering in your mind like a light switch, the decision tree forces you to put the mindshare you would otherwise give to the suffering to a more productive use: making sure you neither unnecessarily suffer in the future nor suffer the same thing you have already suffered more than once. It works like this:

Has the suffering already occurred?

1. Yes.
    a. What are the pros of continuing to suffer after the event?
        i. Are there actually any?
        ii.
        iii.
    b. What are the cons of continuing to suffer after the event?
        i. You lose sleep.
        ii. Your mind is not being spent somewhere more enjoyable and productive.
        iii. Etc.
    c. Having been through the suffering, what have you learned that you can do differently in the future to prevent suffering the same thing more than once?
        i. Spend your mind building out this plan and executing it!
2. No, I just expect it to happen.
    a. Is there anything you can do to make it less likely that this suffering will occur?
        i. Yes.
            1. Spend your mind working through this instead!
        ii. No.
            1. Stop spending any of your mind on this. It's entirely outside your control, so you might as well enjoy the present!

CHAPTER 6 TAKEAWAYS

1. Suffering is an inevitable part of life. While you can lessen it, you can never avoid it entirely.

2. What you *can* avoid is suffering the same thing more than once, whether that means "pre-suffering" before the event even occurs, "post-suffering" by ruminating on some past suffering you can now do nothing about, or both.

3. To limit and even prevent this unnecessary and unhelpful pre- and post-suffering, work through the suffering decision tree to turn that same mental energy into something far more productive: identifying ways to prevent suffering the same thing more than once.

Suffering Decision Tree

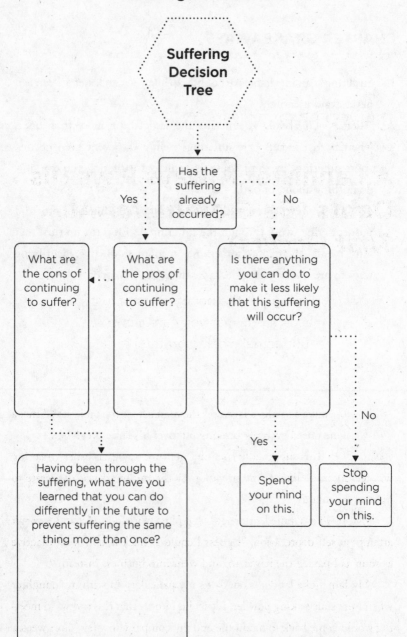

. . . .

CHAPTER 7

A Lannister Always Pays His Debts (*Be Grateful for All That Occurs*)

Recognize the benefits of not just
accepting what you can't control,
but actually being grateful for it.

So, you're actually a lawyer?" the man across the table asked me, a lone raised eyebrow peeking out over his large eyeglasses.

This supposedly friendly "get to know each other" meeting was feeling more like an interrogation by the minute. I was desperate to lighten the mood.

"More like a failed attorney," I replied with a smile and a weak attempt at self-deprecation. "I guess I couldn't hack it, so I went inactive as soon as I passed the bar exam and went into business instead."

My lame joke landed as flatly as my pancakes do with my daughter when I use stale baking powder. Little did I know that this awkward meeting would come back to haunt me and my company in a few short weeks.

I had thought that the meeting was a mere formality and that the good people at the North Carolina Real Estate Commission (NCREC) would see the merits of my position once they got to know *me* and better understood my business. The reality was far murkier.

The more I tried to explain my new company, VacationFutures, and how it was different from listing sites like Airbnb and Vrbo but its revenue model was the same, the more I was met with stone-cold stares and silence on the other side of the table. Worried I was simply digging the hole my company was in ever deeper, I stopped rambling and asked if the NCREC had any further questions for me.

"We will reach out when we do" was the foreboding and toneless reply.

I thanked the men for their time and, with my heart racing, attempted to maintain a seemingly genuine smile as I shook hands and made my way out of the government building. That had not gone at all like I had planned.

Weeks earlier, I had received an email from the NCREC warning me that my business—an online marketplace that connected homeowners with professional vacation rental management companies for their homes—was operating in violation of the rules of the Real Estate Commission in the state of North Carolina. Based on a single email from a property manager who did not like this newfangled innovation in her backyard, the NCREC had determined that my company was illegally acting as a "broker." This term had a specific legal definition and onerous legal requirements to go with it.

When I first received the email, I actually laughed. The NCREC couldn't be serious, right? We were operating an online marketplace and charging fees in the exact same way as sites like Airbnb, Vrbo, and Booking.com. If those other multibillion-dollar businesses were operating within the limits of the NCREC's rules, surely my two-person startup was as well.

I emailed a reply to this effect to the NCREC, and the response I received had me laughing even harder than when I received the first email from them.

"We have never heard of these other companies you mention in your correspondence," the NCREC replied, "but we have heard of you, and so you are the problem."

Initially flattered that my newly formed startup apparently had a larger profile in some quarters than the publicly traded companies I'd mentioned, I was clearly not laughing now. To the NCREC this was no joke, and should it stick to its position, I didn't know if VacationFutures could survive as a business. Thus, thinking my charming personality and ability to make the NCREC see reason would achieve in person what my emails to date had failed to accomplish, I reached out to request an in-person meeting in the belly of the beast. This was the meeting I was now leaving, likely with my case in an even worse position than when I'd arrived.

Less than a week later, my concerns were validated. In a three-page letter outlining its decision, the NCREC referenced my comment about being a "failed attorney" as support for the premise that it would be dangerous to let me continue to operate my business in the state. I would have to change, or the NCREC would fine me and shut me down faster than I could say *LOL*.

I was terrified. This was my first startup. It had taken me nearly ten months to convince my wife to let me quit my lucrative job, and here I was, less than a year into striking out on my own, with my startup apparently destined for the trash heap before I ever managed to get it off the ground. I just stared at the PDF on the screen in front of me, reading it over and over, hoping for some way out.

Eventually, I found it. Perhaps I was not as much of a failure as an attorney as I'd let on.

In one part of the letter, the NCREC justified its unequal treatment of my company and companies like Airbnb, Vrbo, and Booking.com by pointing out that those companies had no basis of operations in the state. Sure, my startup had fewer than one hundred North Carolina homes listed on its website and each of those companies had thousands of properties across the state, but apparently the determining factor in deciding how the NCREC would treat each business was not whether the business made money in the state, or even how much it made, but rather whether it created jobs and paid taxes in the state. The rather backward reasoning led to the conclusion that so long as I did not create any jobs or pay any taxes in the state, I too would be treated in the same manner as those big companies.

The irony of this logic was that the only reason I was even in North Carolina in the first place was that the state had a startup program encouraging companies from the Southeast to relocate there. I had applied for and joined the program only months earlier, and my primary residence and my wife were still based in Atlanta. The weekly commute to Durham was not exactly something either of us looked forward to.

At the same time, my one employee in North Carolina (my only employee at that time) was an entry-level salesperson—a role I could fill just as easily in the 6-million-person Atlanta metro area as in the 270,000-person Durham, North Carolina, area. On top of it all, in the past couple of months, since the NCREC had first reached out, I had shifted the operation of VacationFutures from the pure transaction-based service I'd envisioned to a less efficient and less lucrative subscription basis, in an ongoing (and consistently failing) attempt to appease the powers that be.

Thinking that perhaps I was just reading things as I wanted them to be, I wrote back to the NCREC, wanting their response documented. "Just to confirm," I wrote, "as long as I do not have an office or any employees in the state, it will be OK for me to operate under the same transaction model that you are OK with sites like Airbnb and Vrbo using?"

Before the end of the day, the "Yes" I received in response came through and changed the trajectory of my business and my life. By the end of the month, I'd parted ways with my one North Carolina employee, managed to bring on two more in Georgia, and cut off my weekly roundtrip flights between ATL and RDU. I would have been thankful to the NCREC if the only benefit it had given me was the additional time back at home with my wife.

But the benefits didn't stop there. Because the NCREC's push forced me to rethink my business model, VacationFutures saw hockey stick growth, with transaction volumes and revenue doubling each month. This growth also means that, far from being annoyed by or frustrated with the NCREC, I am incredibly grateful for the push the Commission gave me.

Forever Grateful

This concept of being grateful for our challenges and difficulties was advocated by the Stoics. Thinking through his own hardships in what was his personal journal, Marcus Aurelius wrote in *Meditations*:

'It is my bad luck that this has happened to me.' No, you should rather say: 'It is my good luck that, although this has happened to me, I can bear it without pain, neither crushed by the present nor fearful of the future.' Because such a thing could have happened to any man, but not every man could have borne it without pain. So why see more misfortune in the event than good fortune in your ability to bear it?

For Marcus Aurelius and the Stoics, accepting and learning from events and occurrences was not enough. Limiting the "suffering" to the event itself was not even enough. To make the most of life's challenges, to really be Stoic in the face of adversity, required taking it one step further and being *thankful* for things others would lament.

Nearly two millennia after Marcus Aurelius's rule, the Austrian physician and psychiatrist Alfred Adler explained why this approach works. "Meanings are not determined by situations," he wrote, "but we determine ourselves by the meanings we give to situations."[34] A situation is not "good" or "bad" in and of itself. These labels only come, can only come, through the meaning we give them. As Shakespeare said through Hamlet, "There is nothing either good or bad, but thinking makes it so."

We can remain a mind tenant and let the meaning of a situation be defined for us, or we can be mind owners, proactively dictating what meaning we choose to give it. If we do this correctly, and not only accept what comes but actually go so far as to be thankful for it, we have a newfound superpower. A negative outlook leads us to a more negative mindset. A neutral outlook leads to a neutral one. But a positive view? One of gratitude? That will actually make us happier, and there is science to prove it.

• • • • • •

A 2018 study from Harvard on the subject of gratitude found that "gratitude is strongly and consistently associated with greater happiness. Gratitude helps people feel more positive emotions, relish good experiences, improve their health, deal with adversity, and build strong relationships."[35] And the benefits are not only psychological. Other studies have shown that gratitude is associated with getting better sleep,[36] can boost our immune system,[37] and can even reduce pain.[38] As an added benefit, the practice is self-perpetuating. Researchers at Indiana University found that "the more you practice gratitude, the more attuned you are to it and the more you can enjoy its . . . benefits."[39] More and more studies are showing that those benefits are strong and manifold.

Knowing and understanding the upside of gratitude, we are only being sensible when, like a Lannister, we "pay our debts," to borrow a phrase from a popular book and television series. This can apply to anything from putting a positive spin on an event we would normally label negative, to identifying the help that allowed us to get to where we are in life. This admission that perhaps we didn't achieve all our accomplishments entirely on our own can at times fly in the face of our cultural norms. After all, there is nothing that we as Americans love more than the "self-made man." From Horatio Alger stories to innumerable biographies about businessmen and politicians from humble beginnings, these tales come across as the very personification of the American Dream.

But to fail to identify the assistance we received, intentional or not, chance or otherwise, is to miss out on an opportunity for greater happiness, as the research consistently demonstrates. Besides keeping us from coming across as arrogant jerks, this humility is also more realistic. As Maria Konnikova explains in *The Biggest Bluff: How I Learned to Pay Attention, Master Myself, and Win*:

> Nothing is all skill. Ever. I shy away from absolutes, but this one calls out for my embrace. Because life is life, luck will always be a factor in anything we might do or undertake. Skill can open up new vistas, new choices, allow us to see the chance that others less skilled than us, less observant or less keen, may miss—but should chance go against us, all our skill can do is mitigate the damage.[40]

Your hard work and intelligence helped get you to where you are. Recognizing the role of chance does not diminish the work you put into preparation; it merely acknowledges that the particular opportunity itself, or the lack thereof, is not entirely of your own doing and making. That opportunity, that role that chance played, whether in the form of "bad" luck you overcame or in the form of "good" luck that made your journey that much smoother, is something that is definitionally outside your control. You're not a lesser person for acknowledging this—you're simply on your way to becoming a happier one.

The Luckiest Man in the World

"Alert," Christopher slowly pronounced each syllable. "Severe Thunderstorm Warning for Ascension Parish."

Christopher's mother screamed out loud and rushed from the kitchen where she was preparing dinner.

"Christopher, you can read!" she exclaimed with her arms wrapped around her baby boy, tears streaming down her cheeks. "I knew it! I knew you could do it!"

Christopher was fourteen years old, so in most circumstances his performance would not have been remarkable. But Christopher Coleman did not enter life under normal circumstances. One of seven children raised by a single mother in Gonzales, Louisiana, Christopher was pronounced dead at birth. Eight weeks premature and with an umbilical cord wrapped around his neck, Christopher came into this world not breathing, and the doctor's best efforts were unable to resuscitate him. The hospital staff placed his tiny body to the side, covered him with a sheet, and instead focused their attention on safely bringing his twin sister into the world.

It was only once his sister was out of harm's way herself and had been carried to the NICU that the staff heard the weak and muffled cries from under the sheet.

"My God, that baby's alive!" one of the nurses exclaimed, rushing to uncover Christopher and get him the medical care he required.

But by this time Christopher was estimated to have gone without oxygen for fifteen minutes, and the doctors were certain he had suffered extensive brain damage in the process. Not wanting the young mother to unnecessarily get her hopes up, they warned that even *if* her child survived, he would be severely mentally and physically handicapped for the remainder of his life. By the time the family was discharged from the hospital, the doctors had diagnosed Christopher with cerebral palsy and had suggested his mother place him in an institution dedicated to the care of the severely mentally impaired.

"I could never separate my twins," his mother responded. And this was why, fourteen years later, Christopher was now sitting on the family couch reading the weather alert, to his mother's amazement.

The time in between had not been easy for Christopher or his family. Doing what she thought best for him, Christopher's mother enrolled her six-year-old son in the LeBlanc Special Services Center, a state-run school for the disabled. Believing there was no point in even trying to educate someone with Christopher's level of mental and physical impairment, the staff at the school simply placed Christopher in a corner to stare at a blank wall each day. But Christopher's mother never gave up hope. Although she worked two jobs to support her family and often didn't make it home until 3 or 4 AM, she still found the time to take Christopher to the Cerebral Palsy Center for speech and physical therapy.

Just as importantly, Christopher never gave up on himself. Whereas others' ambitions for him seemed to stop at just developing the ability to communicate, Christopher longingly watched as his twin sister advanced in school, learning to read and later to do math. It was at this time that a seven-year-old Christopher developed his "midnight plan." After all his siblings had gone to bed, after his mom had left for the night to work her second job, Christopher would sneak his twin sister's books from her schoolbag and drag them to the bathroom, where, as the rest of the house slept, he slowly and painstakingly taught himself to read.

And so, here Christopher was, seven years into his midnight plan, and he was finally ready to make his big reveal to his mother. She was ecstatic. Within months she withdrew Christopher from LeBlanc and enrolled him in the local elementary school. When the teachers tested him, however, they found that Christopher's knowledge was anything but elementary and he was already reading and functioning at a ninth-grade level! This created its own challenges as Christopher's mother pushed to enroll him in the local high school instead and was continuously met with stiff resistance. His mother's love and fighting spirit were undeterred, however, and she eventually convinced the high school to admit her son. At every step of his life, people had been telling her what her son could not do or become. She was ready for her "miracle child" to prove all of them wrong once again. And so he did.

High school can be difficult for anyone. The social pressures, the bullying, the cliques—few of us would willingly return to those four fraught years. Imagine, then, what it was like for a wheelchair-bound African American teen in rural Louisiana who had only months before been assumed to be incapable of reading and writing. But the cruelty of his classmates only made Christopher more focused, and more driven to prove what he was capable of. It was that dedication that enabled Christopher to roll across the stage on March 25, 1993, and, at the age of twenty, receive his high school diploma with honors from St. Amant High School, ranking fifth in the class of 360 seniors.

Of course, Christopher didn't stop there. He soon enrolled as a prelaw student at Nicholls State University. Two years later, wanting to prove he could manage life on his own, Christopher transferred to

Southern Polytechnic State University in metro Atlanta, where he eventually received his BS in technical and professional communications. It was through this move to Georgia that I got to know Christopher as my neighbor in our Midtown Atlanta condominium building.

Christopher's story gripped me. Everything he had already overcome would have been enough to break almost anyone, and yet his smile and positivity remained ever present and contagious. Christopher often joined me when I took my dog, Henry, for a walk, and I got to know him better over time. On one such walk, Christopher shared some news.

"I recently came out of the closet," he told me.

"Congratulations!" was my immediate response. I had seen the struggles many of my own friends had gone through to take the same step and thus imagined it was a scary but liberating experience for Christopher as well.

I kept walking with Henry but soon noticed that Christopher had stopped his wheelchair. I turned to see what had happened and saw a perplexed look on Christopher's face.

"What's wrong?" I asked him.

"I guess I didn't expect that response," he replied, and then started wheeling forward again alongside me.

As we continued our walk through the neighborhood, Christopher explained how, after graduating from college, he had built his career as a motivational speaker and coach. His greatest source of speaking engagements, and thus income, was faith-based organizations. His coming-out had placed all of that at risk. It was then that I learned that Christopher's coming-out was not entirely of his own volition. A "friend" had gone through his phone, found some text messages, and threatened to out Christopher to his church unless he paid this "friend" off. Terrified, but believing it was the only course of action he could take, Christopher instead chose to out himself. Almost overnight, Christopher's greatest source of speaking engagements disappeared.

As you might guess by now about Christopher, he was down but not out. Over the next months and years, Christopher built up a new client base, this time focused on the corporate sector. Christopher now counts Coca-Cola, Home Depot, Comcast, Chick-fil-A, Prudential, and even his alma mater, Southern Polytechnic State University, among his past and current clients. But perhaps his favorite clients are some of the sports teams that bring him in, like the NFL's Atlanta Falcons.

"You should see it, Andrew," he told me on one of our walks. "I share my story and these big, strong men just start crying like babies!"

It was on that same walk that Christopher made me truly appreciate the power of gratitude.

"You know," Christopher said after telling me about NFL players' propensity to cry, "I think I must really be the luckiest man in the world. I get to do what I love every single day."

If science hadn't already convinced me to be more grateful, Christopher's example would have provided all the evidence I would ever need.

Writing Your Own *Meditations*

"Gratitude changes you. It elevates your mood. That stress and emotional overload that can make you feel so tired and make your body so achy goes away. It reverses your outlook on the world. It changes how you treat people. More importantly, it changes how you treat yourself," writes American television producer, screenwriter, and author Shonda Rhimes in her essay on the topic.[41]

"Fine, I get it," I can hear you shouting at me from here. "Now what?"

Now it's time to start *practicing* gratitude. Perhaps the easiest, as well as the most well-known, way to do so is through the daily practice of gratitude journaling. Every day, set aside the time to sit down and write out, by hand, three to five things you are grateful for. Some people like to categorize these (e.g., personal, professional, relationship), while others prefer a more free-form style. However, recent research has shown this kind of gratitude practice, while popular, is not the most effective sort.[42] Rather than thinking through things you are grateful for, far more impactful is to have others express gratitude to *you*.

Clearly this is easier said than done. Few of us have fan clubs waiting in the wings to regale us with stories of how grateful they are for us. That being said, there is a way you can experience the benefits of others' gratitude without requiring that they explicitly express such gratitude daily: simply thinking back to a time that someone expressed gratitude to you yields a similarly positive effect. For this gratitude visualization to work, however, you must really dig into the experience and the story around it. Why was the other person grateful to you? What did they do or say to express their gratitude? What did you do or say in response to their gratitude? How did you feel before they expressed their gratitude? How did you feel afterward?

As you relive the story in your mind, write it down. Once the story is on paper, you can revisit it, and relive it, quickly and easily over the course of the next week, month, or longer. The more you dig in to the feeling of others' gratitude, the greater the benefits for you. When you feel the effects of a particular story diminishing or notice that you are struggling to fully relive it, start afresh and think back to yet another example of someone expressing gratitude to you. Write down that story and revisit it for the next few weeks or months. Repeat and refresh as necessary. To help get you started, there is a template at the end of this chapter you can use to launch your own gratitude practice.

As you continue to do this each day and week, it will actually become easier and easier, given the self-perpetuating nature of gratitude. Make sure you don't end up just going through the motions, though. Really take the time, really spend the mind, to think through the rich story behind each of those moments when others have expressed their gratitude to you.

One common question about a daily gratitude practice is when to do it. Some advocate doing it before bed, noting the improved sleep that is associated with this practice. I, on the other hand, prefer to do it first thing in the morning. Doing it early sets the tone for the rest of my day. When I start off grateful, I start off happy, and everything from there just seems brighter and that much better. However, the important thing is less *when* you do it than *that* you do it in the first place, so why not start right now?

CHAPTER 7 TAKEAWAYS

1. Acceptance of your circumstances is not enough. The truly Stoic approach is to be grateful for *all* that comes to you.
2. The benefits of gratitude are many and diverse, and the more you practice gratitude, the more grateful you become.
3. Start a daily gratitude practice. No, really, start right now!

Gratitude Practice Template

Write out the story of a time someone expressed gratitude to you.	Think through the takeaways to make it easier to revisit the story later.
I remember when . . .	1. Before the person expressed gratitude, I felt . . .
	2. This person was expressing gratitude to me because . . .
	3. The highlights of what this person said/wrote/did to express their gratitude were: a.
	b.
	c.
	d.
	4. After this person expressed their gratitude, I felt . . .

Write out the story of a time someone expressed gratitude to you.	Think through the takeaways to make it easier to revisit the story later.
I remember when . . .	1. Before the person expressed gratitude, I felt . . .
	2. This person was expressing gratitude to me because . . .
	3. The highlights of what this person said/wrote/did to express their gratitude were: a. b. c. d.
	4. After this person expressed their gratitude, I felt . . .

Nonattachment to Results (*Focus on the Process, Not the Outcome*)

Reframe the process itself as
the result you are seeking.

We really want to be past la Curva de la Muerte before we see them, mate."

What moments before had seemed like unpierceable bravado in David's eyes now looked far more like unalloyed fear. This wasn't fun and games anymore. It was now a matter of life and death.

For the past thirty minutes I had been chatting away mindlessly with David, a fellow tourist in Spain, as he entertained me with tales of his previous days in Pamplona and all the fun he and his Aussie pals were having. As the event officials opened more gates along the bull-running route, the plaza where we were all initially corralled began emptying. A while before (Was it five minutes? Ten? More?), the friends I was with had moved farther down the route and encouraged me to do the same.

"I'm good," I'd told them with what now appeared to have been misplaced confidence. "I'll stay with David here."

Now my friends were gone, nowhere to be seen, and as David sprinted down the street away from where we had been yukking it up moments before, it seemed as if I was all alone in la Plaza Consistorial. It was time to get going.

To put this into context, it was the second week of July 2003 and I was in Pamplona, Spain, for la Fiesta de San Fermín and the running of the bulls made so famous in the United States by Ernest Hemingway. To maintain some kind of order during an event where up to three thousand insane individuals run alongside unaccompanied fully grown bulls, the event organizers have would-be runners start out in a pen of sorts in la Plaza Consistorial. As the time to release the bulls draws nearer, the organizers open gates along the route, allowing runners to move closer and closer to the stadium and farther and farther away from where the bulls begin their own run.

And it was the announcement, via a rocket blast, that the bulls were out of their pen and had begun their run that had sent my new friend David sprinting away from me. You see, the rocket had a seven-second fuse, meaning that by the time we both heard it, the bulls had been out of their pen, and headed straight toward us, for at least that long.

Oh, and for those less fluent in Spanish, la Curva de la Muerte is literally translated as "the curve of death," and it is known by English speakers in Pamplona as Dead Man's Curve. I will leave it to the reader to imagine how this particular landmark earned its name.

I wasn't a complete idiot, or so I thought. I went into my first running of the bulls with a plan. That plan? To remain ten people deep away from the bulls at any given moment. My thinking was that this was close enough for an "authentic" experience, but enough of a cushion to not make things too dangerous.

As I began to chase after David and round an eerily empty Curva, I was far less confident in my plan. Turning onto Calle de Estafeta, I could see other runners waiting on the edges to begin their own runs. They looked my way, but past me, and as their looks of anticipation turned to terror and they began to sprint away from me in panicked haste, I wondered just how close the bulls were.

And then I found out. With little fanfare they ran right past me—the whole group of them, it seemed. To my right side the bulls trotted past, making their way to the stadium.

"Huh," I thought, "that was an anticlimax."

But the people around me continued running, and before I had time to register that fact, a lone bull ran past, somehow separated from his five friends.* That was when my mind went back to a conversation I'd had with my friend the night before.

"The bulls typically aren't too dangerous so long as they stay together," my friend explained. "Then they'll just run as a herd into the stadium. If they get separated, though, all bets are off. They get scared, and that's when they've been known to turn on the crowd."

Just as my mind was beginning to process this new reality and the dangers it posed, I heard screams, and the sea of runners around me parted. Without realizing what I was doing, I ran straight into a clearing with the lone bull faced directly at me. WTF?

As I turned to run away, because clearly I had a chance of outrunning this 1,600-pound monstrosity in front of me, the bull proceeded to gore a runner who had fallen to the ground at his feet. A rather gruesome picture I would later purchase from one of the professional photographers

---

* I would later learn that he got separated because he had slipped and fallen on the turn at la Curva, which is what made that particular part of the run so dangerous.

perched on the balconies along the running route would show me running like a coward as the bull's horn stretches the skin of the victim's arm in a way that seems to defy physics.

I am the one holding a rolled-up newspaper on the top left while the braver men (holding sticks) on the bottom right work to convince the bull to let the man on the ground go.

Others braver than me, and more knowledgeable in the ways of Pamplona, eventually got the bull off of the fallen runner and headed back toward the stadium. But the run was not over. As we made our way to the stadium, the bull turned on the crowd three more times. Finally, and most dangerously, he turned on a fellow American runner in the tunnel leading into the stadium, goring him several times in the head before fellow runners could get the bull through and into the pen that was his destination.

Eventually, however, the bull was corralled into the proper pen, and I went to meet my friends at a café for coffee, pastries, and epic story swapping.

It had been a close miss, but at the end of the day, I left without a scratch, and with one hell of a story to tell. I had clearly made the right decisions since all's well that ends well.

Or perhaps not. Just because the end result had been a good one did not mean that my decisions and actions leading to that result were not flawed. Had I acted in the same flawed way multiple times, for instance, the chances I would have ended up as the one on the ground with a bull impaling me were high. The quality of the result did not equate to the quality of the process leading to it.

Separating the Process from the Outcome

However much we identify the boundaries of our control, however much we prepare to achieve or avoid a certain outcome, however much we work to turn a crisis into an opportunity and try to limit our suffering to the specific moment, however much we attempt to reframe our thinking to be grateful in the face of adversity, the truth is that there are going to be times when our best efforts simply aren't enough. There will be times when we are working toward a specific objective and we won't be able to reach it. We do things for a reason, after all—if all of our work is in pursuit of a specific objective and we fail to achieve that objective, we've failed, haven't we? Likewise, there will be times when we do not put forth our best effort, when we don't do the right things, like in my incident in Pamplona, and yet we will still somehow achieve the objective we were after. In those instances, we will have succeeded, right?

The Stoics would say absolutely not. They realized that however much time and effort we may put into the cause, however much we may desire a specific effect, the end result is not entirely in our control. If "success" is to be predicated on a specific result, if our happiness is to be entirely dependent upon it, then we have effectively handed over our mind to something completely out of our control.

When you control the process in terms of what and how *you* think and act, you exercise an owner's mindset, but when you focus only on the outcome, you relegate yourself to a mere tenant of circumstances outside your control. For the Stoics, this meant being overly concerned with and attached to the *result* rather than the *process*, and it was something to be avoided. This holds just as true when the results are "good" (i.e., as we hoped for) as it does when things end "badly" (i.e., not as we wished).

As Marcus Aurelius advised himself, "Receive without pride, let go without attachment." As with so much else in Stoicism, this concept of nonattachment is not one on which the Stoics alone had or have a monopoly. A similar concept, and indeed virtue, is a core tenant of many Eastern religions, from Buddhism and Taoism to Jainism and Hinduism. With so much supporting philosophy in various geographical regions and time periods, there must be something to it. And there is.

Can't Read My, Can't Read My, No, He Can't Read My Poker Face

The power, and indeed the necessity, of not getting blinded by the outcome is something Annie Duke knows well. Best known as a champion professional poker player, Duke is also an author of books and articles on behavioral decision science, with an undergraduate degree in psychology from one Ivy League institution (Columbia) and a PhD in psychology from another Ivy League school (the University of Pennsylvania).

While on the World Poker Tour, Duke consistently saw how the better professional players were able to distinguish between the quality of the decisions made during a hand and the quality of the outcome. Less sophisticated players were consistently unable or unwilling to do this.

In fact, this tendency to "look at whether the result was good or bad to figure out if the decision was good or bad" is so common that it has a name: resulting.[43] As Duke came to realize, there are few behaviors more likely to hinder one's development as a quality poker player, and even as a decision maker beyond the table, than resulting.

For a professional poker player, or even an amateur just looking to improve, it's crucial to understand that the quality of the input is not the same as the quality of the output. Poker is a game of odds. A decision that will have your hand winning 83 percent of the time is the right one. And yet, 17 percent of the time you will still lose. Focusing on outcome alone is just as dangerous when we reward and reinforce bad decision making that led to a positive result as it is when we change good decisions and good processes simply because this time around they led to a bad result.

Rather than define "right" and "wrong" by the result, in poker and in life, Duke recommends we instead define them by the input—by the process we followed to get there. This can make negative results less painful, but at the same time we have to also accept that it can take some of the sheen off positive results. Duke writes:

> Redefining wrong allows us to let go of all the anguish that comes from getting a bad result. But it also means we must redefine "right." If we aren't wrong just because things didn't work out, then we aren't right just because things turned out well. . . . Being right feels really good. "I was right," "I knew it," "I told you so"—those are all things that we say, and they all feel very good to us. Should we be willing to give up the good feeling of "right" to get rid of the anguish of "wrong"? Yes.[44]

The danger of not separating the quality of our decisions from the quality of the outcomes is not limited to being beaten in a hand at the poker table.

In fact, in *Think Like a Rocket Scientist*, former rocket scientist Ozan Varol cites just this sort of "resulting" that Duke warns us about in explaining how "success produced the biggest disasters in rocket science history."[45] Having "turned the impossible into the possible when the odds were heavily stacked against the agency," NASA experienced successes that "blunted the most capable minds, and boosted their egos," with eventually deadly consequences. Unlike in a hand of poker, where the outcome of resulting might be the loss of some chips to another player, on January 28, 1986, and again on February 1, 2003, the outcome of this resulting was not simply a lost hand in poker but the loss of fourteen crew members' lives when the *Challenger* exploded upon takeoff and later the *Columbia* exploded upon reentry.

After decades of success, the NASA program was learning the wrong lessons. With each passing launch that proved successful, the institution became more cavalier when it came to safety standards. Rather than seeing the near misses and identifying what was going wrong in the *process* that led to them, the learning seemed to be that since the danger and disaster were indeed averted in the *result*, everything was fine. As Varol points out, this sort of "resulting" worked until it didn't, and the eventual results were tragic.

Shangri-La

It was my first time in Shanghai, and Adrian and I were sitting in the executive lounge at the top of the Shangri-La hotel with an astounding view of the city below us. We had gone to college together and had stayed in touch since, but with his life on the other side of the planet from mine, it was rare that we got to catch up in person.

After college, when so many others had traveled the tested, and indeed worn-out, professional paths after graduation, Adrian Wall had instead set out on his own. He was now a serial entrepreneur, business owner, and operator. In the less than twenty years since we'd graduated, Adrian had founded or helped cofound five companies in a diverse array of industries, including retail and hospitality, media and entertainment, natural resources production, physical commodity trading, and investment advisory and merchant banking. He had also scaled them across five continents. At the time we met, his focus was on bringing to China and other parts of Asia some of the best-in-class New York brands, including Joe's Pizza (Asia), Luke's Lobster (Shanghai, Jiangsu Province, and Zhejiang Province), and Black Tap Craft Burgers & Beer (Shanghai).

It was early 2019, and I was in Shanghai on my way to the Global Leadership Conference in Macau for the Entrepreneurs' Organization (EO). Adrian, though he lived full-time in Shanghai, was at the Shangri-La because he had been hired to speak at a conference there for the Young Presidents' Organization (YPO), and as part of that engagement, the organizers had put him up in the hotel. Not a bad deal.

Catching up over drinks on how things had been going for us, we found it hard to believe that life could get much better. Thinking of the opportunities we'd had, the experiences we were a part of, and everything that still, no doubt, lay before us, we were both in incredibly good places. All of which led me to ask Adrian, someone who I knew had also studied Stoicism, about this idea of nonattachment. It was a question I had struggled with for a while.

"Do you think we just believe in this idea of nonattachment because things are going so well?" I asked Adrian. "It's easy to say we aren't attached to the results when everything is great."

Adrian took a sip of his drink and looked out over the Jing'an District in the distance.

"Or," I went on before he could answer, "do you think we think things are going so well *because* of this idea of nonattachment?"

Adrian looked back at me.

"It's definitely easier when things are going well," he replied. "I'm just not convinced we would think the same way if everything wasn't going so smoothly for us."

We debated the question a while longer but eventually moved on to grab dinner and drinks in the city.

Then There Was 2020

In early 2020, news started coming out about a scary new disease that was ravaging China. Though at the time only a rare few in the United States worried about the implications within our own borders, as I read about what was happening in China, I wanted to check in on Adrian. Knowing that he was a restaurateur, I was concerned not just about Adrian's physical health but also about the economic health of his business.

The news wasn't good.

"All the businesses are hurting big-time," he answered me over WeChat. "But we're doing the best we can to get by."

Adrian was down but certainly not out. As summer began and my own business started to recover, I checked back in to see how things were on his end, hopeful for a more positive response this time, as it seemed China was opening up even faster than the United States. However, the news for Adrian had gotten worse.

"Work is going well," he began, "and business is definitely picking up slowly but surely."

But the positive signs from his business did not prepare me for his next message.

"I'm actually here in the US at the moment," he texted. "Mom was diagnosed with cancer in March, so I flew back to help take care of her."

We stayed in touch through the rest of the year. Throughout, Adrian stayed at his mother's bedside, supporting her and his father through an extraordinarily difficult time. In November, despite the doctors' best efforts, Adrian's mom passed away.

Catching up over Zoom at the beginning of 2021, I was happy to observe Adrian's positive outlook. He had just come off a year when his mom had died and his business had contracted by 50 percent, and at the time we were talking he was locked out of getting back to China, and his businesses, because of onerous travel restrictions.

And yet, Adrian's outlook remained positive. He was excited about a new megadeal he was negotiating with a K-pop star whom he hoped to make a brand ambassador for one of his companies. He was excited about some leadership changes he was making in his own business. And speaking of leadership, he had just been named, along with two others globally, to head up YPO's new Leadership Institute. On top of all this, Adrian was writing and looking to perhaps go back to school to get a PhD in neuroscience. Nothing about the difficult year seemed to have slowed him down; quite to the contrary, he seemed more driven and energized than ever.

I reminded him about our conversation two years before and asked him if he still thought we'd believed in nonattachment only because things had been going so well.

"Absolutely not," Adrian answered emphatically. "I've proven to myself that my belief in nonattachment is not based on temporary success. It's a philosophy for life that carries you through those bad times, because life won't always go your way. If it was only for the good times, I wouldn't be talking to you now."

Becoming Detached

All of this is well and good, but how do you actually separate your mindset from the results? The answer is to focus on the process rather than the outcome. The results are fleeting, and the high we get from them quickly fades anyway. However, if we enjoy the process for the process that it is, the lessons will stick with us.

As five-time Olympian, Olympic medalist, and former world-record holder George Bovell told me of his own athletic results, "The medals were mere trinkets. I wasn't an athlete training my body for a race. I was training my mind, and the reward is the rest of my life." The same can be true in your own life, if you adopt the right mindset.

So how do you step off the hamster wheel after a lifetime of chasing grades, medals, titles, money, accolades, and more? The answer comes in the form of another question: What would be worth doing even if you knew you were likely to fail? What is so important to you that, regardless of the result, it's still worth the process of pursuing? How can you start moving more of your mind and time to these sorts of activities?

Please see the worksheet at the end of this chapter as a starting point for working through these questions. Don't worry too much about stopping everything on the left side of the worksheet at once and working only on the things on the right. Training yourself to focus on the process rather than the result is itself a process, and in working through this process, you will achieve the result.

Spending less of your time and your mind chasing a result, and spending more of both on doing things you have identified as having such a worthwhile process that the result almost doesn't even matter, is a journey. There is no destination. The process is the result.

CHAPTER 8 TAKEAWAYS

1. You learn the wrong lessons if you look only at outcomes and not at the processes that produced them.

2. The fixation on outcomes is called "resulting," and it can have deadly consequences.

3. To begin practicing nonattachment, you should start by exploring the things whose processes are so rewarding and worthwhile for you that the result is almost irrelevant.

The Process as the Result

What are things you do (or don't do) today because of what you believe others will think of you?	What would be worth doing even if no one noticed it, knew about it, or would ever find out that you did it?
e.g., job or industry, title, how you dress	

What are things you do (or don't do) today because of what you believe others will think of you?	What would be worth doing even if no one noticed it, knew about it, or would ever find out that you did it?

PART III
. . . .
Mind Renting and ●urselves

CHAPTER 9

Live Where You Are (*Sow Your Own Seeds*)

> It doesn't matter how green the grass on the other side looks if you're still a terrible gardener when you get over there.

That we all spend too much of our lives handing ownership of our minds to other people, as well as to events and circumstances that are beyond our control, should be evident by now. However, our most habitual and harmful tendency is to actually hand our minds over to someone far closer to home: different versions of ourselves. People who hear voices may be deemed crazy by society, but the truth, if we are willing to admit it, is that we spend almost every waking moment debating with voices in our heads—voices that tell us we should be doing more, that we should have said or done something differently in the past, that we aren't good enough, or any number of other unhelpful things. These are not necessarily always "our" voices—they may sound like a parent, a teacher, or even someone we made up entirely. Regardless of whose "voice" we hear, however, the one speaking is actually just a different, nonexistent version of ourselves. The better we get at identifying and setting the boundaries between ourselves and other people, and the boundaries between ourselves and events outside us and our control, the more important it becomes to tackle the necessary and even more difficult task of wresting back ownership of our mind from the enemy within.

Take, for example, my mindset when I started my career. To say that I worked hard during my tenure as a management consultant at McKinsey & Company is an understatement. I had projects there with partners across the globe who demanded calls with me at times convenient for them. This meant I had projects, spanning several months, for which each day started with a call at 6 AM my time and also included a call at 10 PM my time. I deliberately did not say my day "ended" with that second call, as there was work assigned to me after each call that had to be completed and shared with everyone prior to the next call. It was exhausting.

And I wasn't alone. Many of us at McKinsey found ourselves working into all hours of the night, only to wake before the sun rose in order to get to the office before our clients so we could demonstrate our productivity and our worth. When your company is charging clients what McKinsey charges, you have to prove your value every single day. Or so many of us thought.

Finally, I reached my breaking point. My physical and mental health were deteriorating, and the money, the intellectual stimulation, and, yes, the prestige just no longer seemed worth the sacrifices I was making. McKinsey just didn't seem good for me. I reached out to a mentor, someone more senior at McKinsey, and asked if we could grab breakfast.

Over a plate of scattered and smothered hash browns at Waffle House, I shared my thoughts. I shared my exhaustion, my frustration, and my complete bafflement at what to do or where to go next.

Russell watched me across the table, maintaining eye contact, nodding as I spoke, and replaying critical phrases and feelings I expressed. Clearly, the McKinsey training on active listening was not wasted on him.

When I finished, Russell took a sip of his coffee before responding. Rather than pile on to my woes, adding his own horror stories and laments, as so many at "the Firm" tended to do when these sorts of conversations occurred, Russell instead shared an insight that has stuck with me ever since.

"This is a place that, intentionally or not, selects for 'insecure overachievers,'" Russell said. "Meaning, the people who work here constantly work hard, and do an incredible job, but are also so insecure that they never think it is good enough. This means they just keep working longer and harder."

I nodded. I had never heard the phrase "insecure overachievers" before then, but that was exactly how I would describe myself and my colleagues.

"The thing is," Russell went on, "people who leave McKinsey because the workload is too much, because their hours are unsustainable, or because they can never turn it 'off' when they get home find that no matter where they go, their way of working doesn't change."

I frowned.

"The problem," Russell let me know, "is not McKinsey or anywhere else. The problem is *them*. They are the ones making themselves work like this, no one else. Simply changing where they work will never be enough to change *how* they work."

Like any great mentor, Russell was exactly right, and had said exactly what I needed to hear. It was a painful truth, and one I was too easily blaming on someone or something else. The problem was not McKinsey. The problem was my way of working, at McKinsey or anywhere else I might eventually end up. Until I got that under control, it didn't matter who was signing my paycheck—my life would be a grind.

Why, Exactly, Is the Grass So Much Greener?

This concept of taking your internal struggles with you even when your outside circumstances change, as you may have surmised, is something the Stoics understood long before my career at McKinsey began. As Seneca succinctly put it, "The malady goes with the man." But even he was late to the punch: More than five centuries before he wrote those words, someone complained to Socrates that traveling had never done him any good. Socrates, without missing a beat, replied, "What else can you expect, seeing that you always take yourself along with you when you go abroad?"

The point is that though the grass may have appeared greener on the other side, if the reason my own metaphorical grass was brown and dry was that I was a terrible gardener, then moving to the other side would not magically provide me with a greener lawn. All it would do is enable me to trash yet another yard. And so it was with me and McKinsey, or anywhere else for that matter. Until I was ready to tend to myself and my own mind adequately, no amount of running from or to things was going to allow me to escape the core problem: me.

Even worse, by constantly gazing over the fence at that pristine grass on the other side, I was missing out on all the beauty and potential for the garden immediately under my feet at that moment. How much more could I have gotten out of the garden I was in if I had spent my mind on it rather than on what could be if only I was in some other yard?

As much as I would like to think I was unique in focusing on my neighbor's lawn, the sad reality is that we all struggle with this. A Harvard study found that on average people "spend 46.9% of their waking hours thinking about something other than what they're doing."[46] That's right. Nearly *half* of our lives are mentally spent somewhere other than where we actually are.

If all this daydreaming helped us become happier, healthier, and more productive, that would be one thing. After all, daydreaming is a sign of active thinking, and thinking is what defines us, right? "Cogito, ergo sum" (I think, therefore I am), René Descartes famously wrote nearly four hundred years ago. As it turns out, daydreaming and our resulting happiness are indeed related, but in a way opposite to what you might hope. One of the authors of the Harvard study found that "mind-wandering is an excellent predictor of people's happiness. In fact, how often our minds leave the present and where they tend to go is a better predictor of our happiness than the activities in which we are engaged." The problem is, the same Harvard study found that mind-wandering affected happiness in the inverse direction—and this negative impact on happiness was more than twice as pronounced as the impact of the actual activity a person was doing at the time. As in my own case where I was making myself miserable thinking how my imagined life would be better if only I could escape McKinsey, the study concluded that "this mind-wandering typically makes [people] unhappy." The research suggests that, rather than Descartes's more famous statement, the modern update from Vietnamese Buddhist monk and prolific author Thích Nhất Hạnh is apropos: "I think (too much), therefore I am (not there to live my life)."[47] Indeed.

The Constant Gardener

"What did we just pull off?" Bobby Gibson, the CEO of Travel Keys, asked his COO, Bryan.

The two clinked glasses, drank their margaritas, and looked off into the distance, picturing the bright future that now lay ahead of them.

And what had they pulled off? A coup beyond their wildest imaginings.

At the time, Travel Keys was a tiny company. It had been initially founded as Villas Caribe by Bobby's parents as a way to help luxury homeowners in the Caribbean rent their homes as vacation rentals to well-heeled guests, and Bobby had recently taken over running the business and was bringing it into the twenty-first century.

Whereas the business before his time had focused on things like print ads, Bobby noticed this "new thing called Google," he now says, "where we could be highly targeted, and none of our competitors were yet using it."

His parents were hesitant to make the switch to the untried digital model, but Bobby's conviction led them to cut all print advertising and refocus their dollars on digital ad spend. "It was a little like a glider being pulled up into the air behind a jet," Bobby says. "When the glider disconnected, we had no idea if this thing would work, or if we would fall to the ground and it would be a terrible flaming wreck."

Fortunately for Bobby, the all-in bet paid off. The results of the new advertising strategy were so good, in fact, that Bobby's parents decided to step out of the day-to-day operations and hand control over to him. Looking for other ways he could move Travel Keys into the digital world, Bobby inevitably ended up on the website of the giant of online travel at the time: Expedia. Thinking there might be an opportunity to partner with the online travel agency to package Travel Keys homes with Expedia flights, Bobby sent a form submission to the company through its partnership page. He never expected what came next.

"This was 2005," Bobby says, "and Expedia was just starting to look at the vacation rental space. Remember, this was *years* before Airbnb even started. And so what they did was pull together an advisory council for this segment of the industry so that they could better understand how it was evolving, and ideally identify some potential partners in the process. I show up and the council is a who's who of the industry. It was people like Carl Shepherd [cofounder of HomeAway, now Vrbo, that sold to Expedia for $3.9 billion in 2016] and Ben Edwards [president of the VRMA, the national association for vacation rental managers]. When I stepped into the room, it definitely felt a little like bring-your-kid-to-work day."

But if Bobby was intimidated, he didn't show it. In fact, he soon earned the respect of the other advisory council members, as well as the attention of Expedia. After some initial back-and-forth, including threats by Expedia to work with Bobby's largest competitor instead, the two sides came to an agreement in principle that would give Travel Keys the exclusive right to put its villas on Expedia's site for certain markets.

"Their site traffic was thousands of times what ours was," Bobby says. "I could see the dollar signs before we even inked the deal."

All of which led Bobby and his COO to this dive bar in New York, where they were celebrating their big win. Sure, the yard they were in today with Travel Keys was plenty healthy and green in its own right, but the grass on the other side where Expedia would take them? That was basically the gardens at the Palace of Versailles. They couldn't wait.

But wait they did. While the two sides had been able to agree in principle relatively quickly, agreeing on the specifics took far longer. After eighteen months of negotiation, Bobby and Travel Keys finally signed the megadeal with Expedia that was going to propel the business to new heights. They had pulled it off. But what exactly was "it"?

"What did we pull off?" Bobby poses the question today with the wisdom of hindsight and a totally different tone. "We pulled off an operational nightmare for our company that my team hated, and that over the first year generated a measly three below average bookings in terms of size and revenue. Turns out, our celebrations were a bit premature."

After twelve months of waiting and waiting for Expedia to unlock the huge boost in sales and revenue they had expected, Bobby and his team came to a realization.

We're not going to be able to depend on someone else like that, Bobby remembers thinking. *Only we can make ourselves successful. Let's focus on what we're good at.*

This shift led Bobby and his team to a renewed and laser-like focus on what mattered most to their business: the quality of the guest experience and the quality of the homes they offered.

"We really narrowed our focus to only those markets where we knew we could be the best," Bobby says. "And we went really deep on the guest experience side. How many bookings could our local concierge service actually handle in a month? Yes, more bookings might drive short-term revenue growth, but if the quality of service started to deteriorate, that would have negative effects down the line."

Bobby and his team also looked at their cost of acquiring new customers and found that it was far more expensive to attract new customers than to retain existing ones. This led Travel Keys to put more emphasis on repeat bookings and in turn created higher margins.

"I also realized that if I was ever going to build this into the company I wanted, the company I knew it could be," Bobby says, "we couldn't just focus on a single region."

Bobby's realization led Travel Keys to expand far beyond its Villas Caribe roots and add new homes in places like Hawaii, Central America, US ski markets, Italy, and France.

And all of this added up. Whereas the "megadeal" with Expedia had virtually no commercial impact on the business, this internal focus and execution enabled Bobby to double the growth rate of the business to 30 percent a year and to sustain that accelerated growth for years.

Bobby admits, "2009, on the heels of the financial crisis, was a minor blip, but even then, we were profitable thanks to everything we had done [previously], whereas without that? I'm not sure we would have survived."

The lesson for Bobby was clear, and it was also two-part. First, there was no "silver bullet," and no one else was going to be the white knight who made his business a success. Only the business itself was capable of doing that. The second lesson? That this was not a sprint but a marathon. Building that beautiful lawn with the lush, green grass he had imagined in signing the Expedia deal would not come overnight. Instead, it would come from years of focused and dedicated toil. A decade, in fact.

In early 2017 Bobby's diligence paid off when Accor, one of the five largest hotel chains in the world, purchased Travel Keys for an undisclosed but very healthy eight-figure sum.

"It was rewarding to know that my dad would be set for life," Bobby reflects.

Perhaps even more valuable than the money, though, was the lesson the experience taught him. After purchasing Travel Keys, Accor appointed Bobby as the CEO of onefinestay, Accor's brand for luxury home rentals.

"Even today we are going through many of the same things," Bobby acknowledges. "People internally see all the success Marriott has had with integrating the rentals program with their loyalty program and think it will magically be the same for us."

Bobby demurs.

"I've learned it's not as easy as throwing up some homes on a website," he says. "It's going to take a lot of work on commercialization, the messaging, the booking flow, and more. The real world isn't like *Field of Dreams*. Just because we build it does not guarantee anyone will come. It takes a lot of focus. It takes a lot of work. But that's what makes it fun."

Your Own Green Thumb

There is another version of Bobby's story. One where Bobby decides that the Expedia deal is just not the right deal, or perhaps is not being implemented to its fullest potential. It is a story where Bobby and his team focus outwardly, trying to fix whatever it is that is holding them back from making it to that greener pasture that they imagined Expedia promised.

That story would more likely than not have had a very different ending. Without the renewed internal focus, it is almost impossible to imagine that Travel Keys could have doubled and maintained its growth rate. Without a decade of 30 percent annualized growth, it is doubtful there would have been such a lucrative exit. Without the renewed internal and operational focus, there is a question of whether Travel Keys as a company could have even survived the 2008 financial crisis and its effect on travel, which they weathered so well.

Fortunately for Bobby, his family, and his team, he decided early on that the story of Travel Keys would not be one written by someone else, in which Travel Keys remained a bit player. As a sort of "choose your own adventure," Bobby decided not to go down the path of being someone else's sidekick or riding on their coattails; instead, he wrote his own story and put Travel Keys front and center within it.

The question, then, is, how and where should you do the same in your own life? Where are you now gazing longingly over a metaphorical fence, imagining how much better life would be if only you were over *there*? How do you break this habit, which science shows only detracts from your happiness, and instead get to work tending the garden right below your feet?

The answer is to **SOW** the seeds of your garden:

SOW: Stop, Own, and Work.

First, you must **Stop** looking elsewhere. You now know that looking over the fence at your neighbor's garden will not make you any happier or better off. Why waste your time, and your mind, on it?

Next, **Own** the garden right below your feet. With that extra 46.9 percent of your mind you just got back added to the 53.1 percent of your mind you were already focusing on your own garden, just imagine how much greener you can make your own grass now!

Finally, **Work** diligently to maintain your garden and make it what you want it to be. As with the "overnight" success that was a decade in the making, the secret sauce to a fertile garden, and a fertile mind, is continued and focused effort and work.

To help you get started, please refer to the worksheets at the end of this chapter. It's time to start gardening.

CHAPTER 9 TAKEAWAYS

1. Failing to live where you are is a recipe for discontentment. Whether the grass is actually greener elsewhere is meaningless. All that matters is the grass below your own feet.

2. There is no outside white knight or savior who can or will magically hand you the results you seek. Only you can do that.

3. To cultivate the garden that is your mind and make it bloom effectively, you must first **SOW** your own seeds.

    a. **Stop** looking elsewhere for the solution.

    b. **Own** where you are right now.

    c. **Work** diligently to make where you are the place you want it to be.

Identifying What You Are Seeking and What You Are Seeking to Avoid

What are you currently running *from*?	What specifically about this is the problem?	How are you complicit in making the situation what it is?	What can you do or stop doing to make the situation what you want?
e.g., your boss, the hours you work, your weight			

What are you currently running *from*?	What specifically about this is the problem?	How are you complicit in making the situation what it is?	What can you do or stop doing to make the situation what you want?

What are you currently running *to*?	What specifically about this makes it so desirable to you?	What actions can you take now to achieve or experience the same desired effect where you currently are?
e.g., new job, relationship status, financial milestone		

What are you currently running *to*?	What specifically about this makes it so desirable to you?	What actions can you take now to achieve or experience the same desired effect where you currently are?

CHAPTER 10

. . . .

Live When You Are
(*Be Present*)

There is no past or future you—there
is only the you of right now.

It took me ten months to build up the nerve to quit my well-paying corporate job and commit full-time to VacationFutures, my first company. The idea had initially come to me during a serendipitous conversation over lunch while on a family vacation. Rather than go back to enjoying the beautiful beaches in Turks and Caicos, I ended up spending the rest of that holiday researching the vacation rental industry, the players, the size, and more.

The idea took hold of me immediately. However, quitting my job was a big step not just for me but also for my wife. I had to get her on board with the certainty of my salary disappearing and the uncertainty of there being any upside whatsoever. That took time. Finally, that time came, and I gave notice to my employer.

People often say they accomplish more in the first week they fully commit to their new venture than they did in the entire year preceding it, when they were working on it just as a side hustle. That was true in spades in my case. I hit the ground running, and it seemed nothing could slow me down.

Then, a month in, my former CEO, Mark, reached out to schedule a call. We had a great relationship, and I sincerely respected him and what he had founded and built at my prior company, Axiom. I happily scheduled the call.

The conversation started as you might expect, with Mark asking me how things were going with VacationFutures and saying that everyone missed me at Axiom. It was flattering. Then Mark dropped a bomb.

"We have a client that really needs someone like you to do some urgent work."

I remained silent.

"We are in a tough spot, so we are willing to pay quite a lot."

Crickets.

"It wouldn't be full-time or anything. Maybe just ten to twenty hours a week for a month, tops."

I held my tongue.

"We'd be willing to pay a lot," Mark went on. "Overpay, really."

Then he threw out an astounding number. A number that, as I did the math in my head, if annualized came out to more than ten times what my salary was at the time I left. My mind was spinning. What should I say? What should I do? That kind of money would fund my company for another six months or more, even without outside investment or new revenue coming in.

I did the only thing I could do. I politely declined.

As a founder himself, Mark said he understood. "I think I would make the same decision in your shoes," he reluctantly admitted. "It's probably the right one."

We ended the conversation with him wishing me well, and we went our separate ways.

I imagine many people reading this are thinking either *You're insane!* or *You're a complete idiot!*

Let me explain.

Seneca famously wrote nearly two thousand years ago that "putting things off is the biggest waste of life." I knew this was true in my own case. It had already taken me ten months to build up the confidence, support, and nerve to strike out on my own. I had begun the work and was loving it. Sure, it was terrifying, but it was also gratifying in a way that nothing had ever professionally been for me before.

Mark's offer was incredible. However, I also saw it for what it would truly be to me: a poisoned chalice. One project would more than likely turn into many. Ten to twenty hours a week could easily grow to forty or more. It would be perhaps even more difficult to break my addiction to the lucrative freelance fees than it had been to part with my full-time job.

I had already seen the benefits that complete focus on my venture could bring, and sliding backward, living partially in the past with my old employer, would prevent me from ever fully living in the present I wanted: being the full-time founder of my new venture. Accepting the training wheels that Mark's offer embodied meant I would instead be putting things off, pushing the most important thing back down to second place. That would have been a big waste of my life indeed.

Sure, the price tag was high, but at that time I was not ready to rent my mental space to anyone else. It belonged to VacationFutures fully and wholly. Making that my *entire* present was the only realistic way I saw of not forever keeping one foot or both in the past.

The truth is that we never know how much time we actually have in this life. The sad reality is that "later," when it comes to a dream deferred, turns into "never" more often than into a dream realized. I would venture to bet that every single person reading this has one, if not many, "some-days" that they have been pushing off until "the time is right." I will let you in on a secret: whether it is popping the question to a significant other, becoming a parent, becoming a founder, selling your possessions and traveling the world, or virtually anything else that makes life worth living, the timing will never be "right." There is only one time, and that time is the present.

When it comes to something new or different, it will be scary, and it will seem hard. There is nothing easier than inertia. Why would you possibly dive into an unknown abyss when things are so comfortable and warm where you currently sit? The answer is in the question: it is actually not all that comfortable. If it were, you wouldn't have that desire to do something different, or that itch that constantly pesters you in the first place. The comfort of stasis is merely an illusion, and a rationalization to justify your paralysis to yourself.

The most famous, and perhaps most successful, example of making the "someday" today is that of Jeff Bezos. He had the idea for Amazon, the company that eventually made him the richest person in the world, but was yet to quit his day job to fully commit to pursuing it. The idea, though, would not leave him alone. In the end, he employed what he called a "regret minimization framework."

On its face, the framework is disconcertingly simple for something that had such a big impact on his life, on e-commerce, and on the lives of billions of people across the globe. It starts with a simple question: In X years, will I regret not doing this? As Bezos explained years later, "I knew that when I was eighty I was not going to regret having tried this. I was not going to regret trying to participate in this thing called the Internet that I thought was going to be a really big deal. I knew that if I failed I wouldn't regret that, but I knew the one thing I might regret is not ever having tried."[48]

And Dying in Your Beds, Many Years from Now . . .

Bezos's line of reasoning echoes that of humans more generally. It is not the things that we did that we most often regret; rather, it is the things that we didn't do that haunt us. In fact, this regret was number one in Bronnie Ware's *The Top Five Regrets of the Dying*.[49] When patients were on their deathbeds, their most commonly expressed regret was "I wish I'd had the courage to live a life true to myself, not the life others expected of me." As the author explains, "This was the most common regret of all. When people [realize] that their life is almost over and look back clearly on it, it is easy to see how many dreams have gone unfulfilled. Most people had not [honored] even a half of their dreams and had to die knowing that it was due to choices they had made, or not made. Health brings a freedom very few [realize], until they no longer have it."[50]

All of these regrets stem from failing to live in the present and failing to make the present what we want it to be. Just as we saw that people on average spend nearly 50 percent of their waking hours thinking about something other than what they are doing, this delaying of pursuing the life we want means that much of that time is spent living in not just a *place* other than where we are but also a *time* other than now. We fixate on and replay something that has already occurred, or we fantasize about some future in which we finally have the courage to do what we wanted to do all along.

This is exactly that "waste of life" that Seneca warns us against. As Pierre Hadot writes in his incomparable study of Marcus Aurelius's

Meditations, "Only the present is within our power, simply because the only thing that we live is the present moment."[51] The past is behind us and will never exist again other than in our heads, and even then, it will exist in our heads only if we allow it to do so. Likewise, the future is, by definition, always the future. All that is, is now. This concept is limiting, but within those constraints, it is also empowering. When you only have the present, you can be *fully* present. When you only have the present, you can make the present what you want it to be, and what it should be for you.

The @Kabbitch*

"I've never been a settled person," Kathryn Petralia tells me. "I've just never been a regular person."

Kathryn is the cofounder and former president of Kabbage, a financial technology company that sold to American Express in 2020 for nearly $1 billion; the cofounder of Drum, an online marketplace that raised eight figures in funding out of the gate; and the founder or cofounder of numerous other technology companies. She was also named by *Forbes* as one of the one hundred "Most Powerful Women in the World." I have to agree with her. She is *not* a regular person.

Kathryn decided to quit her own day job at Revolution Money in 2008, which as fate would have it also eventually sold to American Express, to go and found Kabbage. Whereas I had no children when I left to start my first company, Kathryn had a son. Whereas I had a spouse who had a steady income to give our household some financial stability and security, Kathryn was the sole breadwinner in her own house. How did she build up the conviction, the courage even, to make the leap?

_____

* This is Kathryn's actual Twitter handle.

"It wasn't like that was a one-time thing," Kathryn explains. "My entire career, even going back to picking a major in college, has been about seizing the opportunity at the time."

This approach led Kathryn on a nontraditional path, as you might imagine. Struggling to settle on a major, she eventually decided on English. "I liked to read and write," she says, "and my favorite teacher in high school was my AP English teacher. I could see myself as an English professor."

This in turn led Kathryn to pursue a PhD in English literature—a path she followed happily until a friend, the former CEO of Equifax, reached out to ask Kathryn for a favor.

"'You know computers,' he said to me. 'Can you step in and help with this new investment I just made?'" Kathryn says. "And I guess at the time I did know computers. This was the early nineties, when most people had no experience with them, but I had had one since I was seven, so it was more like second nature to me."

Seizing the opportunity, Kathryn said goodbye to academia and jumped on board the startup, a data compression company she describes as "the Pied Piper of the time," for those *Silicon Valley* fans out there. While at the startup, Kathryn says she saw all the catalogues coming through the mail "that companies were spending God knows what to mail out, and that most people threw away without ever looking at them." She thought, *I could put this online.*

Kathryn pitched the idea to the same friend who had recruited her to oversee the data compression company, and he was intrigued enough to invest. In 1995 she launched her first tech startup. From there, Kathryn went on to work at an internet consulting firm, and then on to Compu-Credit, a kind of early version of Capital One. While at CompuCredit, she helped launch Revolution Money, and she eventually left her "day job" to join the financial services startup full time in 2007.

And then in 2008, while Kathryn was still at Revolution Money, another friend reached out to her with an idea. It was Rob Frohwein, a corporate attorney in Atlanta. The idea was to use nontraditional sources of data, like eBay transactions, to make automated lending decisions to small businesses that most banks would not lend to.

Again, never one to think about what might have been, Kathryn responded, "That's a good idea. I can help you with that.'"

"Helping with that" led Rob and Kathryn to build Kabbage, one of the most successful financial technology startups of its time; Kabbage raised $400 million in equity and billions of dollars in debt facilities over more than a decade. Twelve years later, having provided more than $15 billion in lending to small businesses along the way, Kathryn decided it was time to make a move once again.

"With the PPP program [the Paycheck Protection Program launched by the federal government in response to COVID in 2020 to assist small businesses in trouble due to the pandemic], we were actually doing better as a business than we expected," Kathryn says. "We were also doing important work. I don't think I fully realized when we founded Kabbage how important credit is to small businesses and how important small businesses are to the economy. On my deathbed I will never be prouder of anything than I am of what we did in PPP. It was remarkable. I would have never thought I could have that experience lending to small businesses."

But while things were going well, Kathryn also saw a great deal of risk in the world around her. "With millions of people out of work," she says, "I just couldn't believe the markets could keep performing like they were at the time. How could the markets keep climbing when the world was falling apart around them?"

Again, not one to wait and see, or to bemoan what might have been if only she had acted, Kathryn and Rob decided it was time to sell, not just for their own financial security, but also for the good of their clients, who would have the security of a bigger financial institution to support them, and for the benefit of the Kabbage employees, who would share in the lucrative exit.

"There were a lot of people who worked really hard for more than a decade to build Kabbage into what it had become," Kathryn reflects. "We wanted to make sure they got to see the financial benefit of all of that."

All of which led to the sale of Kabbage to American Express on October 16, 2020. So, what's next? Kathryn is not wasting any time. Besides her role with American Express as part of the sale, she and Rob continue to grow their newest venture, Drum, a technology startup still in its early days.

"It might not work out," Kathryn admits, "but it's not like we'll have to ask ourselves what could have been because we never tried."

The Gift at Hand

In the English language, it is no accident that the word *present* can mean both "the current time" and "a gift." The word, and both meanings, originates from the Latin prefix *prae-* (meaning "before" or "in front of") as well as the participial form of the verb *esse* (meaning "be").[52] The present, when it comes to time, is literally before us. It is at hand.

Similarly, the meaning of *present* as a gift originated in Old French from the concept of "bringing something into someone's presence, and hence of giving it to them."[53] In this very real sense, the time before us, the present moment, is a gift. It is likely the greatest gift we can or ever will receive. And yet, because we constantly receive it, we also constantly take it for granted. We prefer to focus on the past or the future, times that by their very definition will never be *now*.

This is not to say that reflecting upon and learning from the past has no place; it does. Nor is it to suggest that planning for the future is unnecessary or undesirable; it can be both. Instead, the point is that the decision to spend your present on times other than the present moment should be a conscious one, and a limited one at that. Should you spend 10 percent of your time reflecting on the past? 20 percent? There is no firm answer. There is only *your* answer, and you need to make sure it is one you consciously make and desire.

The same goes for the future and planning for it. What you have to realize is that all this reflection and planning is time wasted if those reflections and plans are not adequately addressed and acted upon in the *present*. If you spend the majority of your time, or even 46.9 percent of your time, somewhere other than the present, you are effectively giving away half your life to the pre- or post-present you. You have left the present you with only a fraction of your mind, making you a mere mind renter from the past and future you.

Sure, plan for the future, but act in the present. You don't want to compromise your future by not thinking about it and planning for it at all. But neither do you want to give away too much of your life, a life that is actually lived only in the present, because you have spent your entire mind on the future.

There really is *no* time like the present. Make sure you give it your full presence.

CHAPTER 10 TAKEAWAYS
. . . .

1. Life is lived solely in the present.
2. The present *is* a present, meaning a gift, but as it is constantly given to you and familiarity breeds contempt, you are apt to take this for granted and waste the present by dreaming of an uncertain future or replaying a nonexistent past.

3. Rather than put off seizing the opportunity today and waiting for the "right time," you can make the time right now by using the "regret minimization framework" made famous by Jeff Bezos.

Regret Minimization Framework

Deceptively simple. Surprisingly powerful.

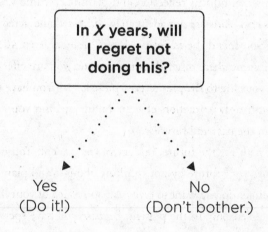

Regret Minimization Worksheet

What do you need to make a decision about?	What might future you regret if you don't do this?	Do it? Don't?
e.g., change job, relocate, relationship		

CHAPTER 11

· ·

Less Is Less, and Less Is Better (*Appreciate What You Already Have*)

Unlock the possibilities of doing,
saying, and wanting less.

'd been up for hours, physically shaking with excitement. Our family tradition, however, was that we weren't allowed to open a single present until the sun was up, and we were all together as a family to unwrap our gifts as a group. Finally, my parents, with coffees in hand, were ready, and my sister and I sprinted to the tree to see what Santa Claus had brought us.

Despite the numerous presents under and around our Christmas tree, my eyes searched for one gift alone: a Nintendo Game Boy. My parents, both pediatricians, were very anti-screen before it was cool to be so. This was 1990, before people really even talked about screen time. Still, my sister and I were limited to thirty minutes of television a day, and even then, only if we read for sixty minutes first. And video games were entirely off-limits.

That is why I had appealed to a higher authority. I knew my parents would never allow me to get a Game Boy, but maybe if I could get a message to Santa directly, he could circumvent their strict rules. And so, it was with a child's unguarded hope and anticipation that my eyes swept the room for the one gift to rule them all.

And then I saw it. There it was. Not wrapped like the other presents that came from family members. This one was sitting to the side in all its grandeur and glory, a direct gift from the Man himself. Thank you, Santa!

I slid up to it and began to open the box immediately. I had in my hand everything I could ever want in life. Happiness and contentment were mine forever!

Fast-forward six months, and with my birthday approaching, the Game Boy had lost its luster. Sega had come out with its own *color* screen competitor, the Game Gear. I *had* to have it. Surely *this* would be everything I could ever want and provide me with perpetual bliss, right?

Adaptability Isn't Always a Good Thing

It's easy to mock the greedy materialism of a child, especially when that child is me, but my own story illustrates something all too common in humans in general. We constantly believe we will be happy *when*. Sometimes that "when" is when we get a material item, like my nine-year-old self believed. Sometimes it's when we receive some kind of award, promotion, or recognition. Sometimes it's when something will end, or something new will begin. The "when" can manifest in infinite ways, but the commonality is that "when" is different from today, and we're convinced that once that "when" arrives, everything will be different and better.

And it often is, at least for a little while. Then we get used to the new "when." It becomes the new normal, and we begin to imagine another and different "when" entirely, one where things really *will* be different this time. This time we really will be happy, and will stay that way, if only we can get to *that* "when." And the cycle repeats.

This is normal. It's part of being human. In psychology this behavior is known as the "hedonic treadmill" or "hedonic adaptation." This is the tendency of all humans to quickly return to a relatively stable level of happiness despite major positive or negative events or life changes. We imagine something will make us happier or, as the case may be, sadder, and in the short term it does. Then time passes, and we adapt because that is what humans do, and we end up in pretty much the same state as we were before. Much like a rodent on a hamster wheel perpetually running but not actually going anywhere, we chase happiness only to find ourselves stuck in the spot where we started.

This psychological reversion to the mean holds just as true for something as mundane as the weather as it does for our dream scenario, and even for tragedy. As Nobel laureate Daniel Kahneman has shown, though midwesterners battling the bitter cold in the winter assume people in sunny and temperate California are happier, the overall life satisfaction is virtually the same for both groups.[54] In an even more surprising study, lottery winners were actually found to derive *less* pleasure and happiness from everyday activities than not just non–lottery winners but even paraplegics.[55] It's like the wine connoisseur who doesn't actually get any more pleasure from drinking a glass of the '96 Chateau Lafite Rothschild than the average Joe gets from drinking a glass of the $20 bottle he picked up at the grocery store, but who does end up getting *way less* pleasure than Joe from that $20 bottle. More doesn't lead to more happiness or more fulfillment. It just makes even less satisfy our more exacting standards.

Path to Riches

Thousands of years before this psychological tendency toward hedonic adaptation had a name, the Stoics identified the problem, as well as the remedy. "It is not the man who has too little, but the man who craves more, that is poor," Seneca wrote. And in inverse, Epictetus instructed, "If you wish to be rich, do not add to your store of money but subtract from your desires." It is not getting what we want that makes us happy. Rather, the path to contentment is through wanting what we already have. Happiness is not something we achieve "when," it is something we can and should have now, with the right mindset.

The Stoics have no monopoly on this truism. Lao Tzu, in the *Tao Te Ching*, instructed, "If you realize you have enough, you are truly rich." Buddhism teaches that all human suffering stems from our desire and craving for something more and different. Writer and theologian Frederick Buechner points out that in Hebrew the salutation *shalom* "means fullness, means having everything you need to be wholly and happily yourself," so that in saying *shalom* to someone you are not wishing them more things, but rather wishing them contentment and fullness with what they already have.[56]

If so many cultures have known this about contentment and happiness for so long, how and why do we still get it so wrong?

This tendency to strive for more does not just apply to what we do and pursue. Just as frequently, and with just as poor results, our minds constantly try and take on more. In a world where there is so much to do, multitasking has become our default way of operating.

Have too much to get done during the workday? Just work through your emails while you're on that Zoom call.

Running a little late? Just do your makeup in the car as you drive to work.

Not loving the phone call with your parents? Pull up Instagram and see what other people are up to while saying "Yeah" and asking "Is that so?" every now and then.

The biggest problem with all of this is not that it is rude, which it is, or even that it can be dangerous, which it can be. The biggest problem with multitasking is that we can't actually do it. As Rich Diviney pointed out in chapter four, and as research consistently demonstrates, human minds are not actually doing multiple things at once. Rather, our minds are just switching from task to task extremely quickly. Despite what we may like to believe, the human brain can't actually multitask. As technology enables us to do more things, as we expect and are expected to do more things, this myth about multitasking has gained more and more prominence. However, it remains just that: a myth.

Fine, you may think. *Tomayto, tomahto. I'm still getting more things done faster.*

But you aren't. Again, according to a *Time* magazine article from two researchers at the Cleveland Clinic, research shows that "repeatedly switching back and forth from project to project, like a hummingbird darting from flower to flower and then back to the original flower . . . is hampering our ability to perform even simple tasks" and "can have an extremely negative impact" on our attentiveness, learning, and mindfulness. In our attempt to do more, we actually accomplish less.[57]

Less but Better

So, what is the answer? As more is demanded of us, in reality or in our imaginations, what are we supposed to do? As priorities pile up and compete with one another, how are we to decide among them?

One place to begin, as Greg McKeown points out in *Essentialism: The Disciplined Pursuit of Less*, is by acknowledging that the very word *priority* initially had no plural form. By definition it was singular. It was the thing prior to *all* other things. For five hundred years, from its entry into the English language in the 1400s all the way up to the 1900s, it remained as such. It was only closer to our own time that we bastardized the term and pluralized it, thinking that through a trick in language we could bend reality to our desires.

Thus, the answer is not more. Just as the Stoics would advocate, it is instead "weniger, aber besser," in the words of the German designer Dieter Rams. Or in English, "less but better." It is not that we need to do, get, or say more. It is just that we need to do, get, and say *better*. As research shows, the surest path to this is to do, get, and say *less*.

This is a lesson Jack Dorsey knows well. From the outside, his life would seem to go completely against this principle. As the cofounder and simultaneous CEO of *two* multibillion-dollar public companies, Dorsey would seem to be the embodiment of just how successful multitasking can be.

The truth is that Dorsey did not start Square while he was still at Twitter. At the time, he was actually in exile from the company. He was all in on Twitter and then all in on Square. As each started, it had his full and undivided attention. And while it is true that he is now the titular head of both companies, the fact is that Jack Dorsey is such a strong proponent of the idea that less is better that he describes his role as CEO as being the "chief editor" of the companies. As he explains, "By editorial I mean there are a thousand things we could be doing, but there are only one or two that are important."[58] His job is not to help his companies identify all the things they *can* be doing, but instead to help them narrow their focus down to the one or two that they *should* be doing.

Fine for his companies, you might think, *but clearly he is at least multitasking himself.* However, here again, Dorsey walks the talk. As McKeown explains in his book on essentialism, Dorsey understands the importance of focus and "has divided up his week into themes. Monday is for management meetings and 'running the company' work. Tuesday is for product development. Wednesday is for marketing, communications, and growth. Thursday is for developers and partnerships. Friday is for the company and its culture."[59] At every point, every single day, Dorsey does less, but does it better.

In this mindset and approach, Dorsey is in good company. As the master innovator of our time, Steve Jobs, put it, "Focus means saying no to the hundred other good ideas . . . I'm actually as proud of the things we haven't done as the things I have done. Innovation is saying 'no' to 1,000 things. You have to pick carefully."[60] Or as Ray Dalio, founder of the world's largest hedge fund, writes in his book *Principles: Life and Work*:

> While you can have virtually anything you want, you can't have everything you want. Life is like a giant smorgasbord with more delicious alternatives than you can ever hope to taste. Choosing a goal often means rejecting some things you want in order to get other things that you want or need even more. Some people fail at this point, before they've even started. Afraid to reject a good alternative for a better one, they try to pursue too many goals at once, achieving few or none of them. Don't get discouraged and don't let yourself be paralyzed by all the choices. You can have much more than what you need to be happy. Make your choice and get on with it.[61]

Which is all well and good to say, but what does this actually look like in practice?

The Cloud Sherpa

Michael Cohn has built not one career but three (so far) on the back of his ability to say no to the good ideas in order to focus on the great one.

As the founder of Cloud Sherpas (acquired by Accenture in 2015), the founding managing director of seed accelerator Techstars Atlanta, and now the cofounder and managing director of the venture capital firm Overline, Michael has seen his fair share of good ideas that he ultimately turned down. However, he admits this practice and discipline did not always come easily or naturally.

"When we started Cloud Sherpas in 2008," Michael says, "we weren't 100 percent sure which direction we were heading, but we could see this huge opportunity Google was creating by offering their consumer apps, like Gmail, to businesses of all sizes. We reached out to Google saying we wanted to partner with them to resell their software, and though they were at first hesitant, we ended up being one of the first five partners licensed to resell and support Google Apps."

This led Michael to build Cloud Sherpas into a reseller and consulting business that quickly emerged as the leading partner in the Google Enterprise ecosystem. While out fundraising to help continue to fuel the growth of his company, Michael met a local investor and successful entrepreneur named Jon Hallett. After spending several weeks with Michael, Jon proposed a range of investment options outlining ways they could work together. Perhaps surprisingly to anyone reading this, it was the last of these options that Michael was most excited about: having Jon come in and take over the reins of the business.

"Although the business was growing and our prospects were bright, I was a first-time CEO. There was just so much I didn't know about company building. I wanted to learn from Jon," Michael reflects, "and I didn't want to be the bottleneck to growth."

Jon took over the helm of Cloud Sherpas in 2010. By this time, the company had also begun pursuing a new line of business it called SherpaTools.

"As we were consulting for clients, we began to see a lot of the same problems over and over again," Michael says. "Google was focused on delivering a great end-user experience, but at the time really wasn't focused on addressing the growing challenges of system administrators, so we started building out our own software to solve these problems."

Pretty soon after launching SherpaTools in the Google Marketplace, Cloud Sherpas had forty thousand different domains around the world using the free software it had developed. A clear sign that you can do two things at once, right?

"The problem came," Michael admits, "when we realized we were robbing Peter to pay Paul. To build out and service these tools, we had to pull our consultants out of the field. And yet, having our consultants in the field and billing clients for their time was what paid the bills. It was creating some real financial challenges."

This is when Jon Hallett taught Michael a lesson in focus that he has carried with him ever since.

"We can't do both," Jon told Michael. "Each one is a great business, but they're also different businesses. Keeping them together will hold both of them back. SherpaTools needs to be its own company."

Michael was not convinced. Admitting in retrospect that pride came into play, he felt SherpaTools was as much his baby as Cloud Sherpas and was not ready to kick it out of the nest. Eventually, however, Michael came around, realizing this was just the sort of expertise he had brought Hallett in to provide.

"It eventually clicked for me," Michael says. "You know that saying about a merger or acquisition where 1 + 1 = 3? Well, this was the exact opposite. The whole was less than the sum of its parts. More like 2 + 2 = 3."

Michael remained a sizable shareholder in both companies, but they began to function as two entirely separate and independent businesses.

SherpaTools was relaunched as BetterCloud, which has since gone on to raise more than $180 million in venture capital and is the leading SaaS (software as a service) operations management, or SaaSOps, platform in the world. And without SherpaTools and its product development funding needs holding back Cloud Sherpas, Michael and the team were able to grow the consulting business exponentially into a global enterprise cloud consultancy and make it the leading partner of Salesforce, ServiceNow, and Google before selling it for $410 million in 2015 to Accenture.

"None of that would have been possible if we had kept trying to do both [consulting and building technology]," Michael readily admits. "Each needed and warranted 100 percent focus. At the early stage we were at, there was no way to do that under one roof."

This lesson of doing less to make more has been one that Michael continues to ponder, apply, and learn from.

"With Techstars, we selected ten startups from more than one thousand applications," Michael shares. "Over the course of the thirteen-week accelerator, where we lived alongside the founders [in a pre-COVID world], it became clear about halfway through the program which startups truly had a shot and which did not. Turning my attention *away* from those that were floundering and *toward* those that I believed to be viable venture-backed businesses was not easy, but I was better prepared for it after my experience at Cloud Sherpas."

The same is even more true now that Michael has launched his own venture capital fund with Overline.

"It's still early days at Overline," admits Michael, "and our focus today is on refining our investment criteria and developing a process for portfolio support. There are some harsh realities about 'venture math,' however, that aren't going to change no matter how much value we think we can add. Not all of our investments will be winners. We can only write so many checks, we can only serve on so many boards, and we can only help so many founders. To deliver great returns to our partners, we're going to have to have the discipline to double down on the winners and, unfortunately, allow others to run their natural course."

For someone who has already achieved so much, Michael is still shockingly young. What comes next for him is anyone's guess, but you can be sure that it will be great and that Michael's focus will be 100 percent on whatever it is when the time comes.

Losing What You Already Have

In a world where we are all predisposed to seek more and more, how do we even begin to shift our thinking to valuing and prioritizing less instead? How do we stop chasing after the things we don't yet have and instead focus on appreciating the things that are directly in front of us? The answer comes in a specific form of the *futurorum malorum præmeditatio* (negative visualization) exercise we discussed in chapter four.

In *Meditations*, Marcus Aurelius described the most relevant flavor of this exercise for our present purposes: "Think not so much of what thou hast not as of what thou hast: but of the things which thou hast select the best, and then reflect how eagerly they would have been sought, if thou hadst them not."

To begin, make a list of the things you have and value today. You can use the template at the end of this chapter as a starting point. This can include material possessions, your career, the people you love, your health, and more. The list does not have to be exhaustive, especially to start, but make sure you are including things you actually do already have, value, and care about.

With your list in hand, start contemplating each item one by one. Imagine you no longer have this item. For example, if you start with your job, imagine how you would feel if your company shut down tomorrow and you were left without it. If you are considering a loved one, imagine they have passed away and you can never have another conversation with them. If you are thinking about a possession, imagine that it breaks or is stolen and you have no way to replace it. Stick with one item at a time, and really dig into the visualization. Feel everything you would feel if that situation came to pass.

And that's it! Regardless of the item, material or otherwise, that you have just contemplated, chances are that the next time you see or even think about that item from your list, you will do so with a fondness that was previously lacking. As they say, absence makes the heart grow fonder. This actually holds true for imagined absence as well. Imagining the absence of the people, events, and things that we may take for granted can allow us to derive far more joy and pleasure from them today, before we have lost them, and can help us stop wasting our mind and time chasing after things that won't make us any happier in the long run anyway.

CHAPTER 11 TAKEAWAYS

1. Thanks to hedonic adaptation, chasing after "things," material or otherwise, in the long run won't make you any happier.
2. Given this truth, the surest path to happiness and success is not to pursue more, but rather to appreciate what you have and to focus your limited time and mind on less. Choose the single great thing over the many good ones.
3. To develop this way of thinking, a form of the Stoic practice of negative visualization can help.
    a. Create a list of the things you have and value today.
    b. Think about the items one by one; imagine how your life would be if you lost each item.
    c. Revisit each item with a newfound appreciation and joy.

Negative Visualization Worksheet

List the things you already have and value.	Describe how you feel about them after having "lost" them in your visualization.
e.g., loved ones, professional status and/ or accomplishments, possessions	

List the things you already have and value.	Describe how you feel about them after having "lost" them in your visualization.

CHAPTER 12

. . . .

Lower Your Bar (*Avoid the Perfection Trap*)

A counterintuitive approach can
help you achieve better results.

I frequently receive requests to mentor budding entrepreneurs, and I try
to accept as many as I have time for. In one such conversation, a first-
time aspiring founder, Alison (not her real name), wanted to know
more about my background, the jobs I'd held prior to starting Rented, and
the journey thus far in the company's development. She was trying to map
out my path as a template for her own, which I advised her against doing.
I firmly believed, and still believe, that one must make one's own path.

In playing back what she heard me say, Alison paraphrased my outlook in the following terms: "It sounds like you think people should do
what's right for them."

"I don't think that's it," I replied. "I think that rather than do what's
right for them, people should *do*, and then make what they have done right
for them." I sincerely believe the distinction is far more than semantics.

So many people think that there is a "right" answer and that the hard part is identifying that singular truth. They find themselves frozen, unable to move forward for fear that they aren't making the perfect decision or taking the perfect action. Experience shows that this mindset is terribly misguided.

The world is far too complex to allow for singularly right or wrong answers to difficult questions. Rather than to seek the perfect answer, the goal should be to find a good answer with the information available, and then to do what is necessary to *make* it a great answer after you make the decision in question or take the chosen action. As with ideas for companies and products, it's not the initial idea of the answer that makes the difference most of the time—it's the execution of that idea, and the perseverance in pursuit of that answer when times become difficult.

A good example of this is Facebook. It was far from the first social network. At the time of its launch, websites like MySpace and Friendster had far more users and engagement than the now globally dominant player. Facebook as a social network was just another good idea. But then Mark Zuckerberg and the team *made* it great by what they *did* with that idea from there: they got unrelenting pull demand for their specific social network by slowly and deliberately rolling out campus by campus to college students; they created a social graph that identified how and to what extent people were connected with one another and were able to tap into it to sell advertising in a newly targeted way; they switched their focus to mobile just as that platform became the dominant one; they acquired future would-be competitors like Instagram and WhatsApp; and more. The lesson being, there was no single "right" answer. Rather, they chose a path, and then through their subsequent actions, made it the right answer for them.

Analysis Paralysis

With the information overload we all experience, weighing our options can quickly lead to analysis paralysis. Rather than helping us get closer to a great answer, we remain stuck in place, never coming to an answer at all. In the words of Marcus Aurelius, the important thing is to actually make a decision, start a course of action, and at that point "persevere then until thou shalt have made these things thy own."

Writing closer to our own time, Harvard psychology professor Ellen Langer explains:

> Generating more questions will not help, because there is no logical stopping point. We might just as well pick a moment to stop asking questions, recognize that it is an arbitrary moment, and then make a gut decision. We can then work on *making the decision right rather than obsess about making the right decision* [italics added].[62]

This is not to say that there should be no analysis or filtering. Rather, it is about recognizing that at a certain point the analysis has diminishing returns and can actually have negative effects. That point is likely far earlier than you realize.

A study by psychologist Robert Rosenthal illustrated the power of focusing on making the decision right rather than overanalyzing in search of the "right" answer in surprising circumstances. Demonstrating what has since been called the "Rosenthal effect," he showed that telling teachers ahead of time which students were identified as having higher IQs and were labeled "intellectual bloomers" actually led to this becoming fact. The students who the teachers were told were smarter at the beginning of the year actually did become smarter at a faster rate than the rest of the students in the same classes, as measured on the same IQ test given at the beginning and end of the year.

That is all well and good, you might think, *the IQ test and labeling were both spot on*. However, that's not the end of the story. The names of the students who were labeled as "intellectual bloomers" were chosen *at random*. These students' IQs were no higher than the rest of the student' IQs at the beginning of the year. The fact that the teachers merely *thought* that these students were smarter and would be more adept at learning led to intellectual advancements for those same students. The teachers were not given "exceptional" students, but the teachers' belief that these students were gifted made the teachers persevere in educating these students into "intellectual bloomers." Even without realizing it or intentionally trying to do so, we seem entirely capable of persevering until we have "made these things our own," just as Marcus Aurelius instructed.

Pursuit of the Minimum Rather Than the Maximum

In the world of startups, the cult of the "MVP" reigns supreme. First popularized by the book *The Lean Startup*, "MVP" in this context does not refer to the award that inevitably seems to go to Tom Brady after each Super Bowl, but rather stands for "minimum viable product."[63] In the words of Eric Ries, the book's author, "The minimum viable product is that product which has just those features (and no more) that allows you to ship a product that resonates with early adopters; some of whom will pay you money or give you feedback."[64]

This definition may be a mouthful, but at its core is acknowledging the necessity and indeed advantages of lowering the bar for the first version of a new product. By doing this, you can get it out sooner, get real customer feedback sooner, and start improving it in the right way more quickly. In other words, make the decision and then subsequently work to make the decision right.

Your first product will not be anywhere close to your final one or your "best" one. Your true best first product will be not some idealized, perfected version cooked up in your own head, but the one that you can get out the door most quickly, and most cheaply, because the best product you can produce at that time will be the one that is good enough and that you can get into the hands of actual customers immediately. Only then will you get real feedback and insight on how people actually feel about what you have created. When people are asked what they think about a new product or idea in a survey, it's easy for them to lie. Indeed, this dishonesty may not even always be deliberate or conscious on their part, as the "intention-behavior gap," wherein people fail to turn their intentions into actions, is a well-documented phenomenon. When people are asked to part with cold, hard cash, however, the truth comes out more readily.

This is why a common admonition at startups is "Don't let perfect be the enemy of good." As hip and trendy as the phrase may now seem to those in the tech world, the truth is that the phrase itself has deep, historic roots in the writings of the eighteenth-century French author Voltaire, who stated, "Le mieux est l'ennemi du bien." This translates to "the per-fect *is* the enemy of the good" [italics added]. The author of masterpieces like *Candide* wasn't trying to encourage himself or anyone else with this phrase; he was merely stating a fact.

As consumers, we become so accustomed to the versions of products that eventually emerge that we often forget what things looked like in their early days. For a refresher, visit the Wayback Machine at Archive.org and check out what Facebook looked like in 2004 (at that time, thefacebook.com), and see on the next page what Amazon looked like in 1995. Compare that to what they are today. The founders of both companies knew the importance of getting *something* out into the world because only then would they know how to make it better and better. It was only through this quick and iterative process that they were able to build two of the most valuable companies in the world.

[thefacebook]

login   register   about

Email:
Password:

login   register

Welcome to Thefacebook!

[Welcome to Thefacebook]

Thefacebook is an online directory that connects people through social networks at colleges.

We have opened up Thefacebook for popular consumption at:

BC • Berkeley • Brown • BU • Chicago • Columbia • Cornell • Dartmouth • Duke
Emory • Florida • Georgetown • Harvard • Illinois • Michigan • Michigan State
MIT • Northeastern • Northwestern • NYU • Penn • Princeton • Rice • Stanford
Tulane • Tufts • UC Davis • UCLA • UC San Diego • UNC
UVA • WashU • Wellesley • Yale

Your facebook is limited to your own college or university.

You can use Thefacebook to:
- Search for people at your school
- Find out who is in your classes
- Look up your friends' friends
- See a visualization of your social network

To get started, click below to register. If you have already registered, you can log in.

Register   Login

about   contact   faq   advertise   terms   privacy
a Mark Zuckerberg production
Thefacebook © 2004

Welcome to Amazon.com Books!

*One million titles,
consistently low prices.*

(If you explore just one thing, make it our personal notification service. We think it's very cool!)

SPOTLIGHT! -- AUGUST 16TH

These are the books we love, offered at Amazon.com low prices. The spotlight moves **EVERY** day so please come often.

ONE MILLION TITLES

Search Amazon.com's million title catalog by author, subject, title, keyword, and more... Or take a look at the books we recommend in over 20 categories... Check out our customer reviews and the award winners from the Hugo and Nebula to the Pulitzer and Nobel... and bestsellers are 30% off the publishers list...

EYES & EDITORS, A PERSONAL NOTIFICATION SERVICE

Like to know when that book you want comes out in paperback or when your favorite author releases a new title? Eyes, our tireless, automated search agent, will send you mail. Meanwhile, our human editors are busy previewing galleys and reading advance reviews. They can let you know when especially wonderful works are published in particular genres or subject areas. Come in, meet Eyes, and have it all explained.

YOUR ACCOUNT

Check the status of your orders or change the email address and password you have on file with us. Please note that you **do not** need an account to use the store. The first time you place an order, you will be given the opportunity to create an account.

Compare the attitude of those founders to that of some of the better-known tech flameouts, who instead took the approach that they had to deliver a full and final product to market. Webvan was probably the most infamous example of the anti-MVP approach from the first dot-com era, burning through more than $1 billion in less than two years before having to shutter its doors in 2001. And proving that even if history does not repeat itself, it certainly rhymes, six months after launching the short-form video-streaming service Quibi, and after raising nearly $2 billion along the way, founders Jeffrey Katzenberg and Meg Whitman shut its doors. In both cases, the bar was so high internally for what must be brought to market on day one that there was a complete unwillingness, and even an inability, to get an early version of the product out in order to test the idea with the market to see if anyone really wanted it, or what "it" should be in the first place.

The irony in both cases is that each company was founded and built by people who should have known better, and at one time clearly did. Louis and Tom Borders, the founders of Webvan, had initially founded and sold the company Borders Books while still students at the University of Michigan. At that time, they were not hung up on building some idealized version of what their business could be; they just started a business and improved it from there. As the CEO of eBay from 1998 to 2008, Meg Whitman took the company from a little-known website with $4 million in annual revenue to $8 billion in a decade. With Quibi, she forgot those early lessons—she knew what the early version was but got so used to what it became that the company didn't get customer feedback until it was too late.

Perhaps in both cases, having already achieved so much success and holding themselves to a higher bar, these founders could not come to terms with later lowering their bar again. They would have been embarrassed to do so. And yet, as Reid Hoffman, the founder of LinkedIn, the cofounder of PayPal, and an early investor in companies like Airbnb, has said, "If you're not embarrassed by the first version of your product, you've launched too late."

The Supreme Bar

"How did you create such a successful blog?" I heard one of my table-mates ask the man sitting next to me. We were at a conference, about to sit on a panel together, but before we went up all the panelists were having dinner together.

"Well," the man next to me answered as politely as possible, "I just started blogging and did it every day. At first no one visited the site but me, but then, over time, more and more people came, and as they did, there was a lot of content already there. So I guess I built my blog . . . by blogging."

When it comes to the crippling pressure of perfectionism, few are more familiar with this feeling than artists. Whether it's the paralyzing intensity of a blank canvas, a white screen with a lonely blinking cursor, or a song yet to have a single note, "writer's block" is not for authors alone.

This is something my neighbor at that dinner table knows well. Simon Tam is an artist extraordinaire. The founder and bassist of the Slants, Simon is also an award-winning author of the memoir *Slanted*, a composer who has written and starred in his own off-Broadway show, a speaker, an activist, and an organizer. Simon is perhaps even better known as the named plaintiff in the landmark Supreme Court case *Matal v. Tam*, in which he fought for the right to name his band "The Slants"; the court unanimously decided in his favor, thus expanding civil liber-ties for minorities. Throughout his work, whether it is artistic creation or community activism, Simon is committed to not letting perfect become the enemy of good, and thus stand in the way of real action.

"This paralysis in pursuit of perfection," Simon shares, "is common with a lot of musicians. You're working on something like an album, and you get so hung up on the perfection of the end product, the album, that you never get anything done. You get so caught up on the end product as a whole that you never begin the very first thing, playing a single note.

"The same is true with writing. The book may end up being seventy thousand words, but it all starts with just one word. This is why so many bands get stuck just playing covers, or writers end up taking paid one-off assignments from other people. But in the end, the final product is just an accumulation of a lot of smaller pieces. The book, the album, the finished painting, all are the proverbial elephant. The only way to eat it is a bite at a time."

This is a mindset and approach that Simon has put to use on numerous occasions throughout his creative career.

"When you start adding other people in," Simon explains, "it gets even more difficult. Every person in the group may have their own vision of what that end product should be. It's really easy to let those creative differences stop you all from ever taking that first step."

With their United States Supreme Court oral arguments set for January 18, 2017, Simon and his bandmates knew this was a risk they couldn't take.

"We really wanted to have a new album out before orals," Simon explains. "There was this firm line in the sand, and we had to work back from that."

But even knowing they had a deadline looming, some band members were not feeling the muse.

"It's a funny thing," Simon reflects. "We don't expect a plumber to wait for some kind of inspiration to fix our clogged toilet. We don't expect the surgeon to wait for a muse before operating on us. That's just what a plumber or a surgeon does. What's a musician? Someone who creates and plays music. What's a writer? Someone who writes. So get to work!"

Get to work Simon and his bandmates did, creating what they came to call "Slants Camps."

"The one rule was you had to show up with an idea," Simon explains. "It didn't have to be a great idea or even a good one. We didn't have to use it in the final product, but you had to bring an idea."

In these camps, the band members would break into groups, some working on lyrics, others working on musical components, and then they would come together to further refine what each group produced.

"We didn't have time to wait for inspiration," Simon shares, "and I don't believe inspiration spontaneously arrives anyway. Inspiration comes *through* the work, not before it."

The result of these camps was that the band created nearly thirty new songs by the deadline, far more than they needed. Whittling that down to just their best creations, the Slants released the first of what became two EPs on January 15, 2017, three days before they stood before the Supreme Court.

Simon knew the approach would work because it always did.

"This wasn't our first time working in this way," Simon admits. "Our six other releases before that one had all come about with a predetermined drop date. We wouldn't wait for an album to be completed and then schedule a tour to go promote it. Instead, every time, we'd schedule a tour to promote a new album and then work back from there to make the album in time."

"It's a bit strange," Simon reflects. "When we work for someone else, we show up and we do the work. And yet, as creatives, we constantly seem to be able to make excuses for ourselves as to why we can't start the work *now*. At the end of the day, excuses, no matter how powerful, don't get the work done."

Perfect Is a Verb

We often think of *perfect* as an adjective describing an end state. It tells us what something is. However, it's far more useful to focus on *perfect* in its verb form, not as a state of being but rather as a process of *becoming*. This shift allows us to lower the bar in a way that emphasizes the start, not necessarily the finish.

Explaining the difference between lowering "the bar" and lowering her "standards," number-one *New York Times* best-selling author Gretchen Rubin writes, "'Lower your standards' suggests that I'm embracing mediocrity; 'lower the bar' suggests that I'm clearing away hurdles."[65] Lowering the bar is not about expecting or accepting less or worse. It is about enabling better by ridding ourselves of these hurdles, imaginary or otherwise. It's about quieting that noisy perfectionist whose sole objective seems to be not to make us better, but rather to prevent us from ever getting started with anything new or interesting in the first place.

Perhaps surprisingly, the solution to overcoming this inner voice, whether in work or our personal life, in our creative endeavors or our practical commitments, is to think more like a scientist. Specifically, it is to treat more decisions and actions as experiments to be run, tracked, and tested—not as final decisions that are to be set in stone. The way to do this is to follow the scientific method using the following steps (there is a worksheet at the end of the chapter to help you get started):

1. Identify the **question** you are seeking to answer or the decision you are trying to make.
2. Make a **prediction** on what the answer is or the action should be.
3. Develop a **step-by-step plan** to test whether this prediction is correct.
4. **Observe** what you find at each step.
5. **Document** what you find and learn from those findings.

6. Draw a **conclusion**.
7. **Repeat** as necessary.

This methodology works just as well for writing a novel as for testing a new prescription drug or deciding whether or not to make a career change. For instance:

1. Question: Does fictionalizing my childhood make for a good autobiographical novel?
2. Prediction: Yes.
3. Step-by-step plan: Start writing.
4. Observe: Reread what you wrote. Share your writing with people you trust for feedback.
5. Document: Would I want to read this if it was not about me? Does anyone ask for the next chapter because they are hooked?
6. Conclusion: Yes/No.
7. Repeat: New question: Is it the underlying story or how I am telling it that needs revision?
8. And so on.

Remember, the point of all this is to get started and to no longer remain frozen. But in doing so, we shouldn't necessarily lock ourselves into a predetermined track. When Marcus Aurelius says, "Persevere then until thou shalt have made these things thy own," he isn't telling us to blindly push on when it makes no sense to do so. To persevere is to work through the process of making these things *your* own. Only you can decide what that means and what it entails. Fixating on someone else's version or vision of something can be just as damaging and unhelpful as locking in on some previously imagined version of your own making. Through testing and experimentation, you can continue to learn, to iterate, to refine, and indeed to perfect (verb), all in your pursuit of the more perfect (adjective). Now, put on your lab coat and get started.

CHAPTER 12 TAKEAWAYS

1. Perfect is the enemy of good, often serving as an excuse for not doing something at all rather than a motivating force to do something better.

2. To overcome "analysis paralysis" or freezing in the face of a blank page, start by lowering the bar to determine what the first step needs to be.

3. To lower the bar without lowering your standards, iteratively work through the scientific method.

   a. Ask a **question**.

   b. Make a **prediction**.

   c. Build a **step-by-step plan**.

   d. **Observe** the results as you work through your plan.

   e. **Document** the results.

   f. Draw a **conclusion**.

   g. **Repeat** as necessary.

Scientific Method Worksheet

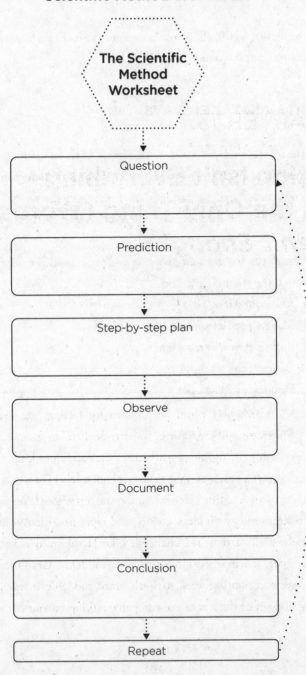

The Scientific Method Worksheet

Question

Prediction

Step-by-step plan

Observe

Document

Conclusion

Repeat

CHAPTER 13

· ·

Action Isn't Everything— It's the Only Thing (*Words Aren't Enough*)

Move from thinking and talking
to action and results.

nyone? . . . Anyone?"

Perhaps I could be forgiven for feeling like Ben Stein monotonously repeating "Bueller? Bueller?" in front of a bunch of teenagers while being met with blank stares and smacking chewing gum. But I wasn't a fictional eighties high school teacher—I was the CEO and founder of an "exciting" tech startup. A startup whose team meetings used to be brimming with ideas, energy, and rapid-fire discussions.

Somehow all of that had changed. Like Hemingway's description of bankruptcy, it happened gradually, then suddenly. Gradually, fewer people were contributing week to week, until suddenly it was just me standing in front of the rest of the company, talking on and on, with no audible agreement, disagreement, or indeed engagement of any sort from my team.

This certainly hadn't been the plan. Lots of companies talk about their employees taking an "owner's mindset." I wanted to take that a step further. Why stop at mindset? Why not make every single employee an actual owner of the company? So that's what I did, awarding stock options to every employee, regardless of role or tenure. I also made it a point to share that the initial idea for the business had come to me because I was an outsider to the industry. I explained that it was because I wasn't tied to years of operating in an established way that I was able to think creatively about how things *could be*. The company where we all worked was the result. But now, having worked for years in that same industry, I had become an insider.

"It's less likely that the next great and innovative idea will come from me," I continuously told the team. "It's going to come from one of you."

And that's why we held these team meetings. That's why we had a virtual "idea board" where people could contribute new ideas and then pitch them each week to the team. That's why I was always so excited to begin each week, because I never knew what people would contribute or where it would lead. And that's also why I was so confused and frustrated when these same meetings had turned into a monologue delivered by me for the third consecutive week. At a loss for what else to do, I adjourned the meeting. Everyone went back to their desks, but I couldn't shake my disappointment in my team. They were letting the company down through their disengagement. They were letting me down.

Over lunch that afternoon I shared my concern with one of my direct reports, expecting her to share my frustration or at least understand it. Instead, her response stopped me in my tracks.

"Why are you surprised?" she asked me.

If I had been surprised before, my face showed I was even more surprised by her question.

"You shoot down every idea anyone brings up. Everyone is scared to speak up because they know you'll just attack them."

I was shocked. I was dumbfounded. What was she even talking about? I wanted to defend myself; I wanted to go on the counterattack against her and the rest of the team. Clearly, they were wrong! But I held my tongue and eventually we finished lunch and went back to work. There I looked at a sign I had handwritten and put above my desk two years prior, after reading a book about Zen Buddhism. It read, "Other people aren't the problem." I had some work to do.

The thing was that in my mind I had never shot down a single idea. I had never attacked anyone, and no one had any "rational" reason to be fearful of my response. After all, how many times had I *told* them how much I wanted and valued their contributions?

No matter what I said, though, my actions were apparently telling them a different story. You see, my training is as an attorney. In law school, our approach to hashing out legal reasoning was for one person in class to throw out an argument and for the rest of the class to try and break that argument down. If the class succeeded in tearing that idea apart, then we moved on to another idea and did the same, and so on, until we settled on the "answer." No one took this process personally because the idea was separated from the individual. This was just how we developed our thinking as law school students. This might also explain why so many attorneys are annoyingly argumentative.

In the business world, or at least in my company at that time, filled as it was with idealistic innovators and creators, the situation was different. Whether or not I explicitly said the idea and the person were two different things, the person who came up with the idea typically saw them as one and the same. Thus, my approach to responding to new ideas and suggestions with "no, and here's why that won't work" was about as inspiring to the people I depended upon to innovate as telling them unequivocally that their ideas, their opinions, and they as humans held no value whatsoever for me or for the company. My entire approach to eliciting feedback and new ideas was undermining exactly what I was trying to achieve. The problem wasn't other people's sensitivity or their reaction to what I said and how I acted. The problem was *me*. As Seneca wrote, "Crimes often return to their teacher." This crime lay firmly at my feet. Perhaps I was more like Ben Stein than I had realized.

The Walk and the Talk

We often think of inspiring leaders in terms of their lofty rhetoric. Whether it's Winston Churchill speaking on the wireless as German bombers wreak havoc across London skies, or Dr. Martin Luther King Jr. sharing his dream from the National Mall during a time of unrest in the United States, or William Wallace stirring up the sons of Scotland before battle as he rides his horse back and forth in front of them, we look to words and the emotion behind them for our inspiration. And yet, words are fleeting. Words are the sugar high that moves and motivates people only for a short time. As is said of parenting, "Kids won't always do as you say, but they will always do as you do."

This is why the Stoics, despite their often incredible writing, knew that words were nothing in and of themselves. Ownership of your mind is worthless unless you do something with it. As Marcus Aurelius reminded himself, "Just do the right thing. The rest doesn't matter."

Action is hard. It is much easier to say or write something than to consistently do the same, to live the same. And this is why, at the end of the day, action really is the *only* thing that matters. It's so important exactly because it's so hard.

In the corporate world, famous examples of this disconnect between words and actions are rampant. "Respect, Integrity, Communication and Excellence" was the motto of one Houston-based energy company. That is, until Enron got caught up in one of the worst accounting scandals in US history and its epic collapse turned the company into a byword for corporate greed and corruption.

"Elevating the world's consciousness" was the guiding mission of another company. Again, that is until people finally began to look past the words of the coworking company WeWork's founder and CEO and started noticing his self-dealing and nepotism.

A "revolutionary" technology that requires only "1/1,000" the amount of blood normally needed for testing was how founder and CEO Elizabeth Holmes described the prized Edison machine created by Theranos. That is, until a whistleblower notified the world that the company's claims weren't true and that it was actually just using other companies' testing equipment to conduct blood tests.

And "an immersive music festival . . . [over] two transformative weekends . . . on the boundaries of the impossible" was how Billy McFarland pitched the now-infamous Fyre Festival on Instagram and elsewhere, until ticket holders arrived in the Bahamas and found themselves without the promised performers and sleeping in FEMA tents.

We have come to take this distinction between words and actions in the business world for granted. Far more companies have mission statements about changing the world for the better than actually work to do so on a daily basis. After all, how seriously can you take a company's words about commitment to the climate if its entire operating model depends on extracting hydrocarbons from the ground to burn as fuel?

And we don't merely expect this divergence between claims and practices. We also seem to derive a sort of perverse joy from seeing these hypocrisies laid bare. The Enron story led to a successful book and movie (both named *The Smartest Guys in the Room*), the Theranos story inspired a book titled *Bad Blood* and an HBO documentary called *The Inventor*, the WeWork story was the subject of an entire HBO series as well as a Hulu documentary, and the Fyre Festival inspired not just one, but two different streaming documentaries. This corporate conflict between words and actions is like a train wreck we're unable to look away from.

And so perhaps we're just asking too much from businesses in the first place. Businesses exist only to make money, after all. Let them say what they want in their polished marketing materials—why should we expect them to have a broader impact and mission? Placing such an onerous burden on them may be where we're going wrong in the first place.

A Not-So-Tiny Mission

Betsy Fore couldn't disagree with this sentiment more. "Every company," she tells me, "is an impact company. The only difference is if it's having a positive or a negative impact, and if it's having that impact intentionally or not."

But Betsy doesn't stop there.

"In the next several years," Betsy predicts, "the *only* companies that are going to be able to survive and thrive are those that are intentional about their positive impact. Society's going to demand it."

When Betsy talks, I listen. Named one of *Forbes*'s "30 Under 30" and the BBC's "100 Most Inspiring Women," Betsy has over a decade of experience as an inventor, product founder, and CEO. She is the cofounder and current co-CEO of the baby and toddler food company Tiny Organics, and she previously founded the pet wearable company WonderWoof and helped build the company Mind Candy (alongside future Calm app founder Michael Acton Smith), which became the top-selling toy brand in the United Kingdom. Across every company, Betsy started with the mission first.

"My son, Sebastian, was born three months before we launched Tiny," Betsy says. "While I was pregnant, I was exiting my last company. It was a really stressful time, but I knew I wanted to get started on my next thing. I just didn't yet know what that next thing was."

That's when she started brainstorming with her eventual cofounder and co-CEO on what they should work on together.

"We knew we wanted to focus on the childhood space," Betsy explains. "That's where my entire career has been focused. From toy companies and games, to "fur babies" [i.e., pets], I've always worked with a focus on making life better and more enjoyable for them."

At a visit to her doctor during her pregnancy, Betsy learned she had gestational diabetes. Already genetically predisposed to diabetes, Betsy began rigorously investigating the nutrition space along with her eventual cofounder.

"The more we looked at it," Betsy says, "the more we realized that the biggest impact we could have on childhood development would be in the area of nutrition."

Having "grown up on a sugar roller coaster in the Midwest," Betsy decided to "reengineer her body" in her twenties and eventually became a vegetarian. It took a while, but eventually Betsy began to see and feel how plants fueled her mind and her body in ways that all of the junk in processed foods never had or could.

"My parents told me my first three words were 'McDonald, Coke, fries,'" she says. "I didn't want that for my son. That's when I decided that the greatest gift I could give him was a love of the food that fuels his body. A true love of vegetables.

"Even after I was a vegetarian for five years, I didn't really love vegetables. I more suffered through them because my adult brain knew they were good for me. Looking into why, I learned we develop our tastes and preferences when we are four to seven months old. That's when [my cofounder and I] realized this could be not only a gift I gave to my son, but also one we could give to a whole generation. What if we were able to get these foods in their hands and mouths at the right age? How could that shape and enhance their entire lives?"

And it was in pursuit of this greater gift that Betsy and her cofounder launched Tiny Organics in 2018. The goal was not just to support a more vegetable-rich diet, but to actually help develop children's tastes so that they'd *prefer* food that is good for them to food that in many ways poisons their minds and bodies. Today, Tiny Organics partners with Michelle Obama's Partnership for a Healthier America in its baby food initiative to support veggie-forward early palate development across the nation. Betsy also personally serves on Mrs. Obama's Shaping Early Palates Board, making sure her own actions, as well as those of her company, match her words.

Such consistency and dedication aren't always easy, but they've certainly been made easier by the fact that this is just how Betsy has always done things, with the mission driving the creation and work of each and every one of her companies.

"It's not just about the start and the end," Betsy shares. "That same consistency in purpose has to carry through with each decision and action."

This consistency was put to the test early on at Tiny Organics: launching initially with a small group of one hundred families in Brooklyn, Betsy learned that being plastic-free was important to the parents.

"No one wanted to pursue this grand vision [of helping their babies live healthier lives] but in so doing contribute to the destruction of the world these healthier kids would then have to inhabit," Betsy explains.

At the time, it would have been easy for Betsy to explain that Tiny Organics was just a food company, not an environmental company. It would have been natural to justify such a position by saying that this was just how the food industry works, and that to get off the ground, the company needed to make some compromises for the time being. This attitude may have been easy and natural for some, but would have been inconsistent for Betsy and Tiny Organics. Had they gone with any of these excuses, Betsy and Tiny Organics' actions wouldn't have been in line with their commitment to making lives better for the children they were feeding. Thus, after a year of trial and error, Betsy and Tiny Organics managed to reengineer the entire chain of production to make it plastic-free, the first of its kind in the world.

"It may seem like a lot of work," Betsy admits, "and a lot of times it is. But cognitively it's actually far easier to stay consistent. If we're clear about what we stand for, about what we're trying to achieve, then that actually provides a pretty solid road map and framework for any important decision. Knowing you're making the right decision makes even the most difficult actions so much easier."

Two Ears and One Mouth

I had dug a deep enough hole with my team that I knew I would have to address the problem head-on.

"I've been a hypocrite," I admitted in the next team meeting. "I told all of you I wanted to hear your ideas, but when you shared them, I focused on breaking them down instead of building them up."

Scanning the room, I could see no one was yet willing to make eye contact with me.

"I know that just telling you I won't do that anymore isn't going to change anything today," I went on. "I know I have to earn back your trust. I just wanted to let you know that I'm committed to doing just that."

I stopped speaking, letting the uncomfortable silence fill the room. It would be great to say that after thirty seconds the team started flooding me with new and innovative ideas. Great, but untrue. No one shared anything that week, or the next. Over the next several weeks, however, as I stopped being the first to speak during the normal course of work after someone said or shared something, and instead remained silent, listening and providing space for others to weigh in, people slowly but surely became more comfortable speaking up. My employees got braver about sharing ideas that may have still been only half-baked.

Once again, the change came gradually, then suddenly.

One idea Tanner shared with me over a coffee at a nearby Starbucks led to the company growing its annual revenue by an astounding 51X over three years, and landed it on the "*Inc.* 500" list two years in a row. Another idea, from Jason, transformed how we did our reporting and financial performance tracking, allowing us to detect problems earlier and saving us millions of dollars in the process. Yet another idea, from Solanda, changed how we did our company goal setting, making the process far more collaborative and transparent for all involved. And still other ideas, ranging from the entirely new business made possible by something Cliff came up with, to the process that made that same business scalable thanks to Karen's work, continue flowing in and flourishing as I write this.

Practice in Action

Not too long ago, my daughter woke me up early on a Saturday morning and asked me to get her purple coat down out of the closet. This being June in Atlanta, I was perplexed. Earlier that week, however, I had noticed a picture posted on her preschool's Instagram account that showed that one of the practical life skills activities the children were doing was buttoning. When I'd asked Talulla that day if she had done any buttoning, she'd said, "No. It's too hard."

Taken aback, I'd proceeded to spend the following week showing her all the things that were hard for me, and that I had to practice. How I worked on my Mandarin each and every morning because it was hard. How I worked on my health by going to the gym every single day and came back sweaty because the workouts I did were hard. How I had to write out what I would say and wanted to learn ahead of any meeting or conversation because forgetting was easy and remembering was hard. I'd showed her over and over how very little was actually easy, and how nearly everything was hard and required practice.

And so, even though I wanted to just roll over and go back to sleep on that Saturday morning and tell her to do the same, I instead asked Talulla why she wanted her coat so badly.

"To practice my buttoning, Daddy," my four-year-old responded. "Because buttoning is hard, and when something's hard, we practice."

Bridging the Gap

Intuitively we all know the importance of "walking the talk." Any daylight between our words and our actions dents our credibility with others, and likely over time erodes even our own self-respect. However, knowing that the two should match and consistently ensuring that they do so are as different as theory and practice can be. The gap is indeed so common that psychology has a term for it. The "value-action gap" describes behavior in which our actions fail to match our stated values.

To start closing this gap and to prevent further gaps in the future, we must identify what we want to match in the first place. Only then can we ascertain where it doesn't yet do so, and from there take on the even more difficult work of making sure it does so going forward. This is where the Bridging the Gap exercise can be helpful.

Start by identifying five core values that you profess to hold. Then, for each of these values, identify a time, ideally as recently as the past week, when your actions did not strictly adhere to your stated value. Finally, work through the following for each value:

1. What about the action didn't match the stated value?
2. If the action had matched, what would it have looked like instead?
3. Can you identify a similar, and similarly difficult, circumstance in which your action did in fact match your stated value?
4. Using question 3 as a starting point, what could you do or stop doing today that would make your action or actions more closely match your stated value going forward?
5. Each day over the next week, track this value—notice when it's tested and how you respond. Work through questions 1–4 daily until you have an entire week when there is no mismatch between your "walk" and your "talk," before moving to the next stated value.

At the start, this exercise and process can provide a difficult mirror to hold up to yourself. Over time, however, by putting the necessary work in, you'll be so much happier with what you see in that reflection.

As we discussed at the beginning of this book, the path to mind ownership is simple. It's about identifying our boundaries, policing their borders, and valuing ourselves accordingly. As simple as this may seem when written on the page, you and I both know it is and will be far from easy. In fact, it's going to be hard as hell. Reading about it, thinking about it, and even talking about it won't be enough. It's going take practice. It's going to take *action*. Now it's time to act.

CHAPTER 13 TAKEAWAYS
• •

1. Talk is cheap. Action is everything, and the only thing that matters.

2. When you are a leader, people won't always do as you say, but they will always do as you do.

3. To identify your own gaps in words and action, and to close them, use the Bridging the Gap exercise.

    a. State the value.

    b. Identify the conflicting action.

    c. Find a circumstance in which you have matched a value and action in the past.

    d. Map how to bridge the gap between the value and action.

    e. Track and refine as needed.

Bridging the Gap

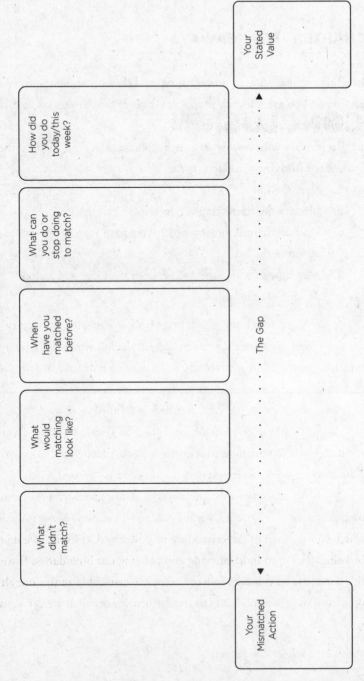

| What didn't match? | What would matching look like? | When have you matched before? | What can you do or stop doing to match? | How did you do today/this week? |

Your Stated Value

The Gap

Your Mismatched Action

CONCLUSION

And what about those things
you just cannot accept?

No justice, no peace!"

Through my mask, I tried to keep up with the chants, but pushing my daughter's stroller up the hill while also having my breathing restricted by my face mask was making it difficult. In the Georgian summer sun, it was also making it very sweaty.

"No justice, no peace!" the marchers continued.

As physically uncomfortable and tired as I was, I looked down at my daughter and remembered why I was there. I looked over at my wife, Katy, and her fierce determination, and I found my second wind.

My belief in the benefits and power of a Stoic approach to life should be clear by now. At its core, for me at least, it's about *owning* my mind, which comes down to understanding its power and its limits. We do this by being clear-eyed in identifying and policing our boundaries. If we do this correctly, we can take full and complete ownership of this one thing that truly and forever belongs to us. By focusing on what we can control and not wasting our time, or more importantly our minds, with the rest, we can make that transition from tenant to owner.

But where is the actual dividing line between what we do control and what we don't? The single best summation is probably that of Epictetus:

> Things in our control are opinion, pursuit, desire, aversion, and, in a word, whatever are our own actions. Things not in our control are body, property, reputation, command, and, in one word, whatever are not our actions.

In other words, we can control our own thoughts and actions—and nothing more. This has been a consistent and powerful guiding principle in my life. But as I looked up at a sign held aloft by a fellow marcher, the words I read made me rethink everything.

Handwritten on a piece of cardboard, the sign bore a quote from Angela Davis: "I am no longer accepting the things I cannot change. I am changing the things I cannot accept."

Whoa. This didn't sound like Stoicism. Doesn't Stoicism focus on recognizing what is outside your control and focusing only on what you *can* control—your mind? Yet, could I disagree with Dr. Davis's words? Did I want to? Didn't they embody what I was doing on this very march? Didn't they represent what I would want from my own daughter and from society in general?

Of course, Davis's statement made me think of another famous quote, this one from George Bernard Shaw: "The reasonable man adapts himself to the world; the unreasonable one persists in trying to adapt the world to himself. Therefore, all progress depends on the unreasonable man."

. . . . . .

Are mind ownership, its ancient roots in Stoic philosophy, and what I have now just spent hundreds of pages advocating all bullshit? Are they nothing more than resignation, condemning us to a life of stasis and mediocrity? This was a question I struggled with for months, and it in fact became the driving force behind writing this book.

On their face, Angela Davis's words seemed in direct contradiction to the principles of Stoicism—after all, Stoicism teaches us to identify our boundaries and to acknowledge that those boundaries go no farther than the limits of our minds. But the more I thought about both Epictetus's and Angela Davis's words, the more I realized how in sync they are. On first read, Epictetus's words are incredibly limiting. The word *control* is so daunting; the bar is so high. After all, what can we possibly control beyond our minds? On the other hand, Angela Davis opens up a world of possibility with her words. Do not be deterred by not having complete control, she says. Go out, and through your actions work to change the things that require change.

Therein lies the true power of ownership. Once you are no longer relegated to renting the remnants of your mind, you are able to *invest* your mind and your time to make more of them, and to dictate where and how you do so. Rather than being distracted by what you don't control, think about what you can influence and how that may ultimately affect what you control and influence going forward.

Dr. Davis's call to action is not anti–mind owner or anti-Stoic, but rather the embodiment of both mind ownership and Stoicism when put into practice. Accepting what you can and cannot control is not the same as resigning yourself to inaction in the face of a wrong. As Seneca wrote in *On the Tranquility of Mind*:

> Even in an oppressed state a wise man can find an opportunity for bringing himself to the front . . . We ought therefore, to expand or contract ourselves according as the state presents itself to us, or as Fortune offers us opportunities: but in any case we ought to move and not to become frozen still.

Just because we can't do or control everything doesn't have to mean that we as mind owners don't have the ability and, the Stoics would argue, the obligation to do *something* to effect the change we want to see in the world.

When I began thinking in this way—about using the principles of Stoicism as a basis for enacting positive change in the world—I started seeing examples everywhere. In my own industry of vacation rentals, property managers in Blue Ridge, Georgia, identified a weekend in September that had the fewest bookings every year. No one seemed to want to visit the area on this particular weekend in September, when summer had officially departed and fall had not yet arrived. The natural thing to do would be to believe that the area was simply not appealing to travelers at that time. Surely the weather; the time of year, which conflicted with work and school; and other factors were completely outside anyone's control, and everyone should just move on.

Fortunately for Blue Ridge, a number of creative thinkers came to the fore. Rather than simply cut their losses when it came to this particular weekend, they realized that they could do something to make the location appealing. They could create new demand by giving people a reason to visit during that time. With this idea in mind, they started a local blues and barbecue festival. The results have been astounding. What started as a throwaway weekend has become an annual festival that not only drives bookings for local vacation rental management companies and property owners and increases the money coming into the local economy, but also creates memories for the families who attend and who look forward to attending each year. The leaders in Blue Ridge used Stoic practices to identify what they could control: what happened in Blue Ridge during that time of year. By investing their minds and time in creating a new event and attraction, they effected the change they wanted to see.

· · · · · ·

Reese Witherspoon serves as another example of someone investing her mind to challenge the status quo. In her thirties, she met with her financial adviser, who commented that her peak earning years were behind her. She was floored. She still had the vast majority of her life ahead of her. Her professional peak was surely some point in the future. Upon further research, however, she realized that the reality, based on the scripts being produced and the roles being cast for actresses her age at that time, told a different story.

Many people would have believed that the industry dynamics were outside their control. Instead, Reese Witherspoon did just as Angela Davis suggested, and decided that the state of the TV and film industry was something she was not willing to accept. She built a coalition of other actresses, began optioning her own scripts, and started producing some of the most acclaimed shows of recent years, including *Big Little Lies* and

Little Fires Everywhere, all built around these women and the characters they portray.

. . . . . .

The answer, then, is not less action, but more intentional action. It is by investing the mind you now own through Stoic action that you will be able to effect changes to things you can no longer accept. To quote Seneca again, "It is not because things are difficult that we do not dare, but because we do not dare, things are difficult." With an owner's mindset, we can and should, as Teddy Roosevelt said and as author and researcher Brené Brown has more recently encouraged us, dare greatly.

Living the Dream

Up until now, we have tackled each of the principles of mind ownership individually, but the reality is that they all support, intertwine with, and feed on one another. While each principle counters a specific manifestation of mental tenancy, it is only by pulling them all together that we achieve true mind ownership. In fact, it is through the sort of daring action that Seneca advocates that we see the perfect illustration of how these Stoic principles can and should be pulled together. In my mind, there is no better example of this cohesive and comprehensive embodiment of mind ownership in practice and what it can achieve than my friend Bernice King.

Dr. Bernice A. King is a minister, an attorney, and the CEO of the King Center. She is also the youngest child of Dr. Martin Luther King Jr. and Coretta Scott King. Throughout her life Bernice has carried the promise and the burden of that tremendous legacy. Through almost unimaginable challenges, most notably the horrific assassinations of her father and her grandmother, Bernice has faced what few of us can even imagine. How she has used these moments as opportunities to learn, to grow, and to effect positive change in society at large is an inspiring illustration of what an owner's mindset can achieve. As we close, two very different stories provide shining examples of how all the principles we've learned about in this book can be pulled together for the greatest effect.

The first story started just as Bernice was named as the CEO of the King Center. Trying to strengthen the relationship between the King Center and the city of Atlanta, Bernice met with then Atlanta mayor Kasim Reed to ask if there was anything she and the King Center could do to help the city. Mayor Reed did not mince his words.

"I wish [the King Center] was more beautiful," he responded.

This was a difficult pill for Bernice to swallow. Housing the final resting place for both of her parents, the King Center was not just her place of work but also the physical embodiment of her parents' legacy. This was hard for Bernice to hear, and her first reaction might have been to tune out the mayor's comments and implied criticism. But what Bernice did instead demonstrates the power of combining the individual principles of mind ownership into a synthesized whole.

Soon after that initial conversation, Bernice saw the fiftieth anniversary of her father's assassination approaching. The King Center was already the number-one destination for international tourists to Atlanta; Bernice knew that on such an important anniversary those tourist numbers would only grow. In the lead-up, however, the King Center did not have the budget for what seemed to be a necessary aesthetic overhaul. What could she do?

First off, Bernice knew her value, and the value the King Center had for the city of Atlanta (chapter one). As the CEO of the King Center and the daughter of Martin Luther King Jr., she could open doors and start conversations others could not.

She also knew her boundaries (chapter two). Bernice recognized the financial limitations of the King Center. It was on fine financial footing for day-to-day operations, but the large capital expenditure that would be required for the center's facelift was beyond its budget. She would have to elicit outside help.

And so, Bernice thought back to the gift of the mayor's earlier criticism of the King Center's appearance (chapter three). There was a kernel of truth in it, of course. Could she leverage that criticism into support in order to remedy the situation?

Not waiting until the fiftieth anniversary was upon her, Bernice planned for the worst ahead of time (chapter four). More than a year beforehand, she began to put a plan in place to get the center ready for its big year.

Rather than lamenting the perfect storm of the anniversary combined with the financial inability to renovate the King Center, Bernice instead turned this crisis into an opportunity to force positive action (chapter five).

In this, Bernice refused to suffer more than once (chapter six). Remember, this was not the anniversary of a birthday or a big speech, but rather the anniversary of her father's *assassination*. This was the anniversary of a tragedy, and one that Bernice had very personally experienced. But being a mind owner, Bernice knew to limit the downside. Yes, the assassination was a tragedy. Its anniversary, however, was now an opportunity to do even more to support her father's legacy and the work he was pursuing when he was murdered.

And so, Bernice felt grateful for the opportunity this anniversary was giving her (chapter seven). It would give her and the King Center an even larger platform to highlight her parents' work and to carry on their legacy.

In doing this, Bernice lived in the here and the now (chapters nine and ten). She didn't dwell on what had passed or waste time daydreaming of what could be "if only." No, she got to work in the present.

Thinking about what work could and should be done, she took a "less but better" approach (chapter eleven), focusing on the most immediately visible part of the King Center: the reflecting pool. Not only is the reflecting pool outside, and thus open to every visitor to the King Center, but it is also the final resting place for both of her parents. She didn't have to redo everything about the King Center. She could start there.

So Bernice lowered her bar to get started (chapter twelve). She didn't go out on a fundraising campaign trying to get millions of dollars to comprehensively overhaul the entire King Center, something that might have taken years and caused her to miss the big anniversary. Instead, she went back to Mayor Reed, thinking back to his earlier criticism, and asked the city for $300,000 to renovate the reflecting pool. Mayor Reed told her he had significant reserves in his part of the city budget and suggested she write a formal request for $500,000. She did so, and eventually the ask was approved in the overall city budget.

As important as all of this was to the center and to Bernice personally, she was able to avoid getting attached to the results, focusing instead on the process and what *she* could control (chapter eight). This made it that much easier to remain undeterred when she got quotes from various vendors to perform the work that all came in several hundred thousand dollars above the $500,000 the city had agreed to provide. The vendors' quotes were outside her control, but how she responded was entirely in her control. And so, Bernice went back to the vendors to negotiate. The project's size and its high-profile nature helped the eventual vendor in turn negotiate better terms with its own suppliers. In the end, this brought the entire project in at $475,000, well within the King Center and the city of Atlanta's budget.

Obviously, none of this came about because of what Bernice said, wrote, or thought. Yes, she did all of those things, but most importantly, she *acted* (chapter thirteen). It was through her action and her perseverance that the King Center got an updated reflecting pool, that her parents got the beautiful resting place they surely earned and deserved, and that visitors to the King Center got a stunning first impression of this monument to Atlanta's most famous son.

As you can see, the story of Bernice's experience with the King Center's reflecting pool is a practical and administrative illustration of mind ownership in practice, one we might each easily relate to, even if on a smaller scale, in our own work and lives. However, the power and the potential of mind ownership in action is far greater than what we saw in that incident, as Bernice's more recent work demonstrates.

In the wake of the 2020 US presidential election, several state legislatures began making moves to change various voting rules, changes many saw as thinly veiled attempts to restrict voting access for minorities. However, no legislature moved more swiftly than that of Bernice's home state of Georgia. As the proposed changes were making their way through the Georgia House and Senate, Bernice joined a Zoom call with several other civic, political, faith-based, and business leaders in the state to discuss how they could use their influence to prevent the proposed changes from being passed into law.

"When I got off that Zoom," Bernice tells me, "it really hit me that this is the centrality of my father's work, perhaps the pinnacle of it. Without that voice and that access, we would not have a say in the outcome of our elections, and our government and policies. When you talk about being a tenant rather than an owner, this is exactly it. Someone else sets all the rules and has the power, and you have zero."

And so, Bernice did what a mind owner does. She got to work.

"I started working with Uncle Andy [Ambassador Andrew Young] to communicate with local business leaders behind the scenes," Bernice says. "As we were talking, it clicked for us that the past year had seen the passing of two of my father's colleagues, and giants of the civil rights movement in their own right, Representative John Lewis and the Reverend C. T. Vivian. From John Lewis taking a brick to the head marching across the Edmund Pettus Bridge in the fight for voting rights in Selma, to C. T. Vivian being beaten, bloodied, and jailed on the courthouse steps in the fight for the same, to the ultimate sacrifice my father made, these three men's lives were given to fighting for the exact rights the Georgia legislature was now proposing to take away."

Bernice, of course, knew her own value. She also realized that in this instance that value would be amplified in a unified message coming from the children of all three men, so she reached out to Al Vivian and John-Miles Lewis. They were immediately on board.

Still, Bernice, Al, and John-Miles had to recognize their boundaries. They were not politicians themselves, but their voices had weight, especially with the business community, so that is where they focused their efforts.

Throughout this pursuit, Bernice was coming to terms with a soul-searching criticism. "For so much of my life I was thinking about how I could carve out my own niche," she recalls. "The entire time everyone else was focused on my parents' legacy. It finally dawned on me that my niche *is* my parents' legacy. My niche is being able to tap into that and amplify that because of the respect so many people have for it. *That* is how I can ultimately push for the most positive social change."

In mobilizing, Bernice was getting ahead of the problem. Hoping to stop the bill before it reached the governor's desk, or at least once it got to the governor's desk and before he signed it into law, Bernice began her action plan behind the scenes in preparation for what was likely to come.

This, of course, better prepared Bernice for the crisis when Governor Kemp ultimately did sign the voting changes into law. "My mother's example was the best lesson I could have received," she says. "She showed me crisis doesn't have to be the end of you. You have the ability to turn those crises into stepping-stones for something better."

With the bill passed, Bernice was not about to suffer more than once. Rather than looking back in frustration at what had happened, she, along with Al and John-Miles, took their campaign public with an open letter picked up by news outlets around the country.

Their entire effort was in recognition of and in gratitude for the debts they owed, and that we all owe, to their fathers and that entire generation of leaders who fought to make our country more equitable. "There is no way our voices would have the value they do without the work of our parents," Bernice is quick to acknowledge.

Still, as important as this work is, Bernice recognizes that she cannot get attached to a specific result. "The journey toward the Beloved Community [a phrase used often by Dr. Martin Luther King Jr. to refer to the ultimate objective of the nonviolent movement] is a never-ending one," Bernice admits. "We have an ultimate goal in mind, but we can't control every single step along the way there. All we can do is continue to show up every day and put in that much needed work."

While acknowledging and expressing gratitude for the legacy her parents left her, Bernice also is well aware that she and others must live in the here and now. "The work that entire generation did was incredible," says Bernice. "But as my mother said, 'Freedom is never really won. You earn it and win it in every generation.' Well, our generation is here, and it is fighting to earn it and win it now."

In any given day, week, or month, Bernice could be pulled in a million different directions. Requests for quotes, for speeches, for her writing and her appearance, don't stop. But Bernice understands the power of "less but better." "This is the fight that needs me right now," she says. "I'm all in."

Being "all in," Bernice might find it easy to set an unrealistic and unachievable bar for herself. However, Bernice is well aware that lowering her bar is not the same as lowering her standards. This is why she started the work with a close family friend first. From there it grew to include Al and John-Miles. This is also why she started with a behind-the-scenes campaign first, and only later took things public. By lowering her bar, Bernice was able to get things started sooner and build from there. Over time, doing this has raised the standards for what she can and will achieve.

And of course, all of this culminated in Bernice's action in pursuit of positive social change. "When the Georgia legislature first started talking about what it was planning to do on voting rights, I'll admit I was angry," Bernice shares. "But I had to turn those emotions into positive action. That's what nonviolence is all about. It's about taking the anger and turning it into something that is not destructive."

It's also what mind ownership is all about. As Marcus Aurelius said so long ago, "Waste no more time arguing what a good [person] should be. Be one."

EPIL●GUE

I t's late September 2012, and David Cummings is back in San Francisco. This time, however, he isn't there to meet with potential investors. Since that serendipitous conversation with Bill Gurley three years
prior, David's focus has been on attracting money into his business the
old-fashioned way: from customers.

This week is David and Pardot's "Super Bowl." Held each September
since 2003, Salesforce's Dreamforce conference attracts the entire Salesforce ecosystem to the Bay Area for a celebration of all things SaaS (software as a service). The attendees represent Pardot's ideal customer base,
and this year, as in prior years, Pardot has splurged for a booth that cost
more than half the company's annual marketing budget. The company
sees it as an opportunity to strengthen relationships with existing customers, as well as close some new ones.

The conference is also an opportunity to strengthen relationships with
key partners. And this is why, between shifts manning the booth with
his team, David finds himself in a meeting a few blocks from the conference center, looking out on a surprisingly cloudless San Francisco sky and
an enviable view of the Bay Bridge. The company David is meeting with
is Pardot's largest referral partner, a mammoth public company with far
more marketing heft and site traffic than the Atlanta-based startup. Pardot

negotiated a deal with this partner whereby customers can buy Pardot's products directly on the partner's single invoice. In return, Pardot pays the partner a 15 percent annuity on the revenue earned from these customers.

David is there to meet with his business development contact at the company and discuss how the partnership is going thus far, as well as to explore ways to drive even more traffic, sign-ups, and thus revenue for both parties going forward. Coming off a conference high with several new contracts already signed that day, David is excited and ready to see where this partnership can now go.

But the public company's representative has other things on her mind today.

"What are you even doing?" she asks David before they have so much as exchanged pleasantries.

David's smile stiffens on his face. He isn't sure what she's talking about and is left at a loss as to how to respond.

"Do you have any idea how much money your competitors are raising? You're not going to have a snowball's chance in hell if you continue down the path you're on."

David is taken aback. Here he is, having been advised by one of the world's leading venture capitalists *not* to raise money. Here he is, having spent the past few years growing his business by an astounding 2,000 percent. Here he is, leaving a conference full of customers and future customers who are continuing to sign up with his company in droves, and this partner, the same partner who is so happy to take 15 percent of the revenue his company earns, is now lecturing *him*, telling him he is doing it all wrong?

But this isn't the David of three years prior. This isn't the uncertain entrepreneur who believes he has to follow the rules of someone else's game. This isn't the David who would allow someone else to live rent-free in his mind ever again.

No, David is now someone who has made his own game, written his own rules, and, by every metric that matters to *him*, is doing just fine. He is also someone who has a secret. Unbeknownst to the know-it-all lecturer across the conference table, David signed a deal to sell Pardot for a whopping $100 million the week before. Though the deal itself is still in due diligence, and thus being kept quiet, once it closes, David and his cofounder aren't going to have to give any of that $100 million to some outside investor. This person, herself brainwashed by the "raise and burn" mentality of the Bay Area venture capital crowd, can sit there and tell David all day long how he is failing to play the game, *their* game, properly, but David is no longer listening.

As amicably as possible, David steers the conversation back to the business at hand. After discussing some new ideas on how to further scale their partnership sales, the two part ways with relief, the business development rep no doubt thinking David will soon follow her sage advice. Walking the few short blocks back to the Moscone Center, David has already moved on. It's time to get back to work.

It Takes a Village

Since the sale of Pardot to ExactTarget, and later, the sale of ExactTarget to Salesforce, David has become a fixture—in some ways *the* fixture—of the Atlanta technology scene. Taking to heart Seneca's observation that "there is no enjoying the possession of anything valuable unless one has someone to share it with," David has dedicated his life to sharing the riches he has accumulated.

This, of course, includes monetary riches, through his philanthropy and investments in early-stage companies, as well as his decision to purchase a large office building and found the Atlanta Tech Village as a hub for up-and-coming companies and entrepreneurs. Perhaps even more significantly, though, this also includes the lessons David has shared with aspiring entrepreneurs. As a cofounder of several companies since leaving Pardot, a board member and adviser to many more, and a founding board member of Atlanta's Endeavor chapter, David not only continues to dictate and cultivate where and how he spends his own mind, but also helps budding entrepreneurs dig out of the mind-renting trap that still captures so many.

Inevitably, the more David shares, the more he gains. Again, this is in a monetary sense, with at least two of his companies reaching unicorn status:* Salesloft at $1.1 billion and Calendly at a whopping $3 billion. But the gains also accumulate in a more meaningful sense in his mind.

"I continue to learn and grow so much," David shares. "I think for a lot of founders the sale of their company is the end. What comes after that? If that's the finish line you're racing toward, what's left to do once you reach it?"

David continues to reflect.

"For me, selling Pardot wasn't the end—it was just the end of the beginning."

As this book comes to an end, I wish you the same mental riches. As Seneca said (and, as readers of a certain age may recognize, Semisonic quoted), "Every new beginning comes from some other beginning's end." The beginning now coming to an end is your life up until now, in which you spent your time as a mind renter. This is not to apportion blame or to lament what has passed. That's now behind you. Before you lies a new beginning: the rest of your life. Before you lies the rest of your mind. Only you can give it away, and only you can take ownership of it.

---

* The term *unicorn status* describes a private company valued at $1 billion or more.

You've completed the first step, learning. Now it's time for the next step in your journey, doing. After all, to quote Epictetus, "If you didn't learn these things in order to demonstrate them in practice, what did you learn them for?" I won't claim that it will always be easy, but as my daughter likes to remind me, "When something's hard, we practice." You have the playbook, and now you are ready to be your own coach. It's time to take to the field that is your life.

Hear that whistle? Practice starts now.

ACKN●WLEDGMENTS

I t is strange, and indeed unfair, that a book ends up having one person listed as the author once it goes into print. The reality, as anyone who has ever gone through this process knows, is that there are many people involved in the process and without them a book would not exist in its final form. There is no way I will be able to do justice to those to whom I am indebted, but I will at least try.

First, I have to start with my wife. Katy. Just meeting you helped make me a better person. Tying my life to yours has been the best decision I have ever made. You have supported me in my dreams and helped me pursue them even when you did not completely understand them yourself. Thank you.

To my daughter, Talulla, thank you for inspiring me to work to be better every single day so that I can come ever closer to becoming the father you deserve. This book is one part of that process and that journey.

To my parents and my in-laws, thank you for helping make me who I am and Katy who she is, and loving our daughter so much, as well as for all the help you gave me so that I'd have time to write.

To all the people who allowed me to share their stories in this book, K.P., Ed, Kat, Gary, Rich, Colin, Christopher George, Tom, Christopher Coleman, Adrian, Bobby, Kathryn, Michael, Simon, Betsy, and Bernice, as well as other people who provided individual conversations and mentoring from others along the way, thank you. It is likely obvious, but this is your book. It is your stories that make it shine, and where it fails to do so, that is my fault, as the inadequate scribe, for not doing justice to your incredible living example.

To the influences who set me on my Stoic journey, from those I know well like Morgan Lopes from my EO Forum, who introduced me to the writing of Ryan Holiday, to my good friend and business partner, Mickey Kropf, with whom I have had many a late-night discussion about the same, to those from whom I learn from afar, like Ryan and Tim Ferriss, thank you. Like so many others I imagine reading this, each of you has left an indelible mark on my life, though we have never met. The examples you provide in the lives you live and the wisdom you share through your writing are truly a positive force for good in this world. I cannot thank you enough.

To my HMS&D '03 family, thank you for making me aspire to learn and grow as a student of life from my teenage years on. I vividly remember a conversation with Rick Dewey when I first got to college in the fall of 1999, a conversation that inspired me so much that I immediately wrote my parents a real letter, with a stamp and everything, to express my gratitude that they had created this opportunity for me to get to know and associate with such incredible people. That was just the start. These men have been a constant and positive presence in my life, and I am lucky to have found them when I did. Thank you to Dan Shevchik, Michael Gentilucci, Leif Drake, and Ryan Parmenter, and special thanks to John "Zinger" Persinger, Cory Walker, and Jan Cieslikiewicz for not just reading early drafts of this (and other books of mine) but also being perpetual thought partners in living a better life.

Adam Grant, through your writing I imagine you are a life mentor to many you will never meet. In addition to being thankful for all I have learned from you and your writing and speaking, I am also forever grateful for your generosity, feedback, support, insanely fast responsiveness, and no-filter approach as a writing/publishing mentor specifically. I had an idea, and you helped me navigate the path to turn it into what readers now have in their hands.

To my agent, Connor, as well as Lucinda at Lucinda Literary, you believed in my writing, and that there was a story to tell. You just knew that it was a bigger and better one than I initially envisioned. Thank you for making me think and write bigger and better, and for introducing me to the amazing Daniel Weizmann, who helped me turn that vision into the compelling proposal that became this book.

Matt Holt and the team at BenBella, your belief in this book, and in me, was apparent from the moment we met over Zoom. Matt, you were the first publisher I met, and I told Connor you had set a high bar that would be difficult for others to clear. Needless to say, I never wavered in knowing you were who I wanted to work with. The same is true for the entire team, whether it was Brigid working with me on countless (all incredible) cover designs more than a year in advance or Rachel, Katie, and Jennifer dealing with my seemingly endless questions, my requests to move timelines, and my cluelessness and insecurity as I went through my first publishing process. You have made what I have heard from others can be a nightmare into a complete dream come true. Thank you.

Inevitably I am going to miss people, and I apologize. My life, as you can see from the stories in this book, is the product of so many incredibly fortunate connections I have been able to make along the way. From Mrs. Kaiser in second grade in Birmingham, to Mr. Alexander and Mrs. Lanier in Greenville, to Dr. Miller and Señor Dawson my senior year in high school in Jacksonville, to Charles Ogletree and Christine Jolls in Cambridge in law school, I have had the good fortune to benefit from some of the best teachers in school and in life. The same is true of my coaches, from Peter at BCC, to Brent St. Pierre, to Greg Troy and Larry Shofe, to Tim Murphy and Eddie Reese; it is only on reflection, with my competition days behind me (as well as with the clarity George Bovell helped me achieve), that I realized your legacy to me, and I imagine to all your swimmers, had nothing to do with the times, the medals, or the meets, but everything to do with the way you helped shape me into the person I am. Thank you.

I cannot close without thanking the people of the island of Bermuda, who welcomed me and my family in the midst of a pandemic, and from where I wrote this book. Your receptiveness, kindness, and beauty are all things I will never forget, and for which I will forever be thankful.

And lastly, to Epictetus, Seneca, Marcus Aurelius, and all the OG Stoics who were formulating these ideas thousands of years ago. Thank you for being the light that helps guide the way and for demonstrating that great ideas, and great work, can far outlive the life of their creator.

NOTES

1. Jordan Peterson, podcast with Tim Ferriss, "Jordan Peterson on Rules for Life, Psychedelics, the Bible, and Much More," *The Tim Ferriss Show*, March 2, 2021.

2. Sam Altman, Twitter post, January 25, 2019, 12:03 PM, https://twitter.com/sama/status/1088844809878425600?lang=en.

3. Taylor Swift, "I Forgot That You Existed," on *Lover*, Republic Records, 2019.

4. James Clear, "The Evolution of Anxiety: Why We Worry and What to Do About It," *James Clear* (blog), https://jamesclear.com/evolution-of-anxiety.

5. Shannon Lee, *Be Water, My Friend: The True Teachings of Bruce Lee* (New York: Flatiron Books, 2020), 121–122.

6. Margaret Mead and James Baldwin, *A Rap on Race* (New York: Laurel, 1971).

7. SWNS, "Millennial Dads Have Pathetic DIY Skills Compared to Baby Boomers," *New York Post*, June 6, 2019, https://nypost.com/2019/06/06/millennial-dads-have-pathetic-diy-skills-compared-to-baby-boomers/.

8. Jim Collins, *Good to Great: Why Some Companies Make the Leap . . . and Others Don't* (New York: Harper Business 2001).

9. Viktor E. Frankl, *Man's Search for Meaning* (Boston: Beacon Press, 2014).

10. Frankl, *Man's Search for Meaning*, 98.

11. Frankl, *Man's Search for Meaning*, 118.

12. Frankl, *Man's Search for Meaning*, 119.

13. Marc Andreessen, "The Only Thing That Matters," from his June 25, 2007, blog now posted at Pmarchive, https://pmarchive.com/guide_to_startups_part4.html.

14. Rahul Vohra, "How Superhuman Built an Engine to Find Product/Market Fit," *First Round Review* (blog), https://review.firstround.com/how-superhuman-built-an-engine-to-find-product-market-fit.

15. Laurens Bianchi, "How Hotmail Became a Viral Hit Once," *ViralBlog* (blog), https://www.viralblog.com/research-cases/how-hotmail-became-a-viral-hit -once.

16. Andrew Chen, "New Data Shows Losing 80% of Mobile Users Is Normal, and Why the Best Apps Do Better," *@andrewchen* (blog), https://andrewchen.com /new-data-shows-why-losing-80-of-your-mobile-users-is-normal-and-that-the -best-apps-do-much-better.

17. Jay-Z, "99 Problems," in *The Black Album*, Roc-A-Fella Records, 2003.

18. See, e.g., Sherwin B. Nuland, *The Doctors' Plague: Germs, Childbed Fever, and the Strange Story of Ignac Semmelweis* (New York: W.W. Norton, 2004).

19. *Plessy v. Ferguson*, 163 U.S. 537 (1896).

20. Charles Thompson, "*Plessy v. Ferguson*: Harlan's Great Dissent," *Kentucky Humanities* 1 (1996).

21. "DODReads 2017 Book of the Year—*The Meditations of the Emperor Marcus Aurelius Antoninus*," *DODReads*, January 31, 2017, https://www.dod reads.com/dodreads-2017-book-of-the-year-the-meditations-of-the-emperor -marcus-aurelius-antoninus/.

22. Philip G. Zimbardo, *Psychology and Life* (Chicago: Scott Foresman, 1985), 275.

23. Amy Norton, "Self-Confident Children May Be Healthier as Adults," Reuters, June 19, 2008, https://www.reuters.com/article/us-self-confident-idUS COL95829220080619.

24. Lee, *Be Water, My Friend*, 135.

25. Lee, *Be Water, My Friend*, 136.

26. Lee, *Be Water, My Friend*, 147.

27. Colin O'Brady, *The Impossible First: From Fire to Ice—Crossing Antarctica Alone* (New York: Scribner, 2020).

28. O'Brady, *The Impossible First*, quotes in this section from 96–97.

29. O'Brady, *The Impossible First*, 108.

30. O'Brady, *The Impossible First*, 229.

31. O'Brady, *The Impossible First*, 122.

32. O'Brady, *The Impossible First*, 261.

33. Ryan Holiday and Stephen Hanselman, *Lives of the Stoics: The Art of Living from Zeno to Marcus Aurelius* (New York: Portfolio, 2020), 246.

34. Alfred Adler, *What Life Should Mean to You* (New York: Little, Brown, and Company, 1937), 14.

35. "Giving Thanks Can Make You Happier," Harvard Health Publishing, November 2021, https://www.health.harvard.edu/healthbeat/giving-thanks -can-make-you-happier.

36. Linda Wasmer Andrews, "How Gratitude Helps You Sleep at Night," *Psychology Today*, November 9, 2011, https://www.psychologytoday.com/us/blog/minding-the-body/201111/how-gratitude-helps-you-sleep-night.

37. Summer Allen, "Is Gratitude Good for Your Health?," *Greater Good Magazine*, March 5, 2018, https://greatergood.berkeley.edu/article/item/is_gratitude_good_for_your_health.

38. "Gratitude: How Can You Benefit from the Practice?," Baystate Health, November 1, 2019, https://www.baystatehealth.org/news/2019/11/gratitude-and-your-brain.

39. Christian Jarrett, "How Expressing Gratitude Might Change Your Brain," *New York*, January 7, 2016, https://www.thecut.com/2016/01/how-expressing-gratitude-change-your-brain.html.

40. Maria Konnikova, *The Biggest Bluff: How I Learned to Pay Attention, Master Myself, and Win* (New York: Penguin, 2020), location 4461–4464 [Kindle version].

41. Shonda Rhimes, "Shonda Rhimes on Why Finding Things to Be Grateful for Is Essential," Shondaland, January 22, 2021, https://www.shondaland.com/inspire/by-shonda/a35284661/shonda-rhimes-being-grateful/.

42. Andrew Huberman, podcast, "The Science of Gratitude & How to Build a Gratitude Practice," *Huberman Lab Podcast #47*, November 22, 2021.

43. Annie Duke, *How to Decide: Simple Tools for Making Better Choices* (New York: Portfolio, 2020), 21.

44. Annie Duke, "Redefining Wrong in Poker, Politics, and Beyond," *Behavioral Scientist*, February 26, 2018, https://behavioralscientist.org/annie-duke-redefining-wrong-poker-politics-decisions/.

45. Ozan Varol, *Think like a Rocket Scientist: Simple Strategies You Can Use to Make Giant Leaps in Work and Life* (New York: PublicAffairs, 2020), 249.

46. Steve Bradt, "Wandering Mind Not a Happy Mind," *Harvard Gazette*, November 11, 2010, https://news.harvard.edu/gazette/story/2010/11/wandering-mind-not-a-happy-mind/.

47. Thích Nhất Hạnh, Twitter post, April 25, 2015, 10:21 AM, https://twitter.com/thichnhathanh/status/591970177861849088.

48. Jeff Bezos, "Jeffrey P. Bezos on Courage," Academy of Achievement video, 2001, https://achievement.org/video/jeff-bezos-12/.

49. Bronnie Ware, *The Top Five Regrets of the Dying: A Life Transformed by the Dearly Departing* (Carlsbad, CA: Hay House, 2019).

50. Susie Steiner, "Top five regrets of the dying," *Guardian*, February 1, 2012, https://www.theguardian.com/lifeandstyle/2012/feb/01/top-five-regrets-of-the-dying.

51. Pierre Hadot, *The Inner Citadel: The Meditations of Marcus Aurelius* (Cambridge, MA: Harvard University Press, 2001).

52. Patricia T. O'Conner and Stewart Kellerman, "Is the Present a Gift?," *Grammarphobia* (blog), June 28, 2013, https://www.grammarphobia.com /blog/2013/06/present.html.

53. Ibid.

54. Jason Gots, "Daniel Kahneman: Why Moving to California Won't Make You Happy," Big Think, August 1, 2012, https://bigthink.com/think-tank /daniel-kahneman-moving-to-california-wont-make-you-happy.

55. Philip Brickman, Dan Coates, and Ronnie Janoff-Bulman, "Lottery Winners and Accident Victims: Is Happiness Relative?," *Journal of Personality and Social Psychology* 36, no. 8 (1978): 917–27.

56. Frederick Buechner, *Listening to Your Life: Daily Meditations with Frederick Buechner* (New York: HarperOne, 1992).

57. Dr. Cynthia Kubu and Dr. Andre Machado, "Why Multitasking Is Bad for You," *Time*, April 20, 2017, https://time.com/4737286/multitasking-mental -health-stress-texting-depression/.

58. Greg McKeown, *Essentialism: The Disciplined Pursuit of Less* (New York: Currency, 2014), 156.

59. McKeown, *Essentialism*, 212.

60. Zameena Mejia, "Steve Jobs: Here's What Most People Get Wrong About Focus," CNBC, October 2, 2018, https://www.cnbc.com/2018/10/02/steve -jobs-heres-what-most-people-get-wrong-about-focus.html.

61. Ray Dalio, *Principles: Life and Work* (New York: Simon & Schuster, 2017), 172.

62. Ellen Langer, *Mindfulness* (New York: Da Capo Press, 2014), 197.

63. Eric Ries, *The Lean Startup: How Today's Entrepreneurs Use Continuous Innovation to Create Radically Successful Businesses* (New York: Currency, 2011).

64. Eric Ries, "Venture Hacks Interview: 'What Is the Minimum Viable Product?'" *Startup Lessons Learned* (blog), March 23, 2009, startuplessonslearned .com/2009/03/minimum-viable-product.html.

65. Gretchen Rubin, "Lower the Bar," *Gretchen Rubin* (blog), February 25, 2011, https://gretchenrubin.com/2011/02/lower-the-bar/.

ADDITIONAL SOURCES

Epictetus. *The Enchiridion & Discourses*, trans. George Long (Welwyn, UK: Ukemi, 2016).

Marcus Aurelius. *Meditations*, trans. George Long (New York: Dover, 1997).

Seneca. *On the Shortness of Life*, trans. Aubrey Stewart. 2017. Kindle.

Seneca. *On the Tranquility of the Mind*, trans. Aubrey Stewart. 2017. Kindle.

Seneca. *The Tao of Seneca: Practical Letters from a Stoic Master*, narr. John A. Robertson, 3 vols. Tim Ferriss Audio, 2016.

Holiday, Ryan, and Stephen Hanselman. *The Daily Stoic: 366 Meditations on Wisdom, Perseverance, and the Art of Living*. New York: Portfolio, 2016.

Irvine, William B. *A Guide to the Good Life: The Ancient Art of Stoic Joy*. New York: Oxford University Press, 2009.

Pigliucci, Massimo, and Gregory Lopez. *A Handbook for New Stoics: How to Thrive in a World Out of Your Control; 52 Week-by-Week Lessons*. New York: The Experiment, 2019.

Robertson, Donald. *How to Think Like a Roman Emperor*. New York: St. Martin's Press, 2019.

INDEX

ABOUT THE AUTHOR

Photo by Stephanie
Nicole Photography

Andrew McConnell is the chief executive officer of Rented, Inc., the leading provider of technology, tools, and services that help vacation rental owners and managers make the most from their properties.

Prior to launching Rented, Andrew founded and ran VacationFutures, Inc., as well as Rented Capital, LLC. He is a back-to-back "*Inc.* 500" honoree and Rented is number six on the *Financial Times* list of "Fastest-Growing Companies in the Americas." Prior to beginning his entrepreneurial journey, Andrew worked with some of the world's largest public and private entities as a management consultant at McKinsey & Company and as a director of solutions design at Axiom Global, Inc. His prior experience also includes putting his law degrees to more immediate use at Eversheds Sutherland (US), LLP, and Ashe, Rafuse & Hill, as well as time at Merrill Lynch.

Andrew is active in numerous nonprofit and professional organizations, including Sheltering Arms, Georgia's oldest charity for early childhood learning, for which he currently sits on the board and chairs the Financial Sustainability Committee; the Entrepreneurs' Organization, for which he was an EO Atlanta board member and EO Atlanta Accelerator board member; the Young Entrepreneur Council; Atlanta Tech Leaders, for which he is a founding advisory board member; and Leadership Atlanta, for which he is a member of the Fiftieth Anniversary Class and served as the Leadership Series cochair.

Andrew writes frequently and is a contributor to *Forbes*, *Inc.*, and *HuffPost*, among other outlets.

A former member of the US National Team in Open Water Swimming and an international medalist, Andrew received his AB in history from Harvard University, his JD from Harvard Law School, and his LLM from the University of Cambridge, Trinity Hall.

He currently lives in Atlanta, Georgia, with his wife, Katy, and daughter, Talulla.

"IF YOU DIDN'T LEARN THESE THINGS IN ORDER TO DEMONSTRATE THEM IN PRACTICE, WHAT DID YOU LEARN THEM FOR?"

- Epictetus

Get out of your head and over to MAndrewMcConnell.com for more tips and tools to put these Stoicism principles into practice.

There you will find additional resources, video, and guides beyond this book to develop and maintain an owner's mindset.

This practice is more effective (and more fun) when you are part of a team, so share your progress, sticking points, and successes with Andrew and others using #getoutofmyheadbook

 @MaMcConnell   /mandrewmcconnell   @mandrewmcconnell

MAndrewMcConnell.com